THE SECRETARIAT OF THE UNITED NATIONS

SYDNEY D. BAILEY

BOOKS (Author)

A Short Political Guide to the United Nations. London: Pall Mall. New York: Praeger, 1963.

The General Assembly of the United Nations. London: Pall Mall. New York: Praeger, revised and enlarged edition, 1964.

British Parliamentary Democracy. London: Harrap. Boston: Houghton Mifflin, second edition, 1962. Arabic edition in preparation.

Naissance de Nouvelles Démocraties. Paris: Armand Colin, 1953.

Parliamentary Government in Southern Asia. London: Hansard Society. New York: Institute of Pacific Relations, 1953.

Ceylon. London: Hutchinson's University Library, 1952.

BOOKS (edited)

Aspects of American Government. London: Hansard Society, 1950.

Parliamentary Government in the Commonwealth. London: Hansard Society. New York: Philosophical Library, 1951.

The British Party System. London: Hansard Society. New York: Praeger, second edition, 1953.

Problems of Parliamentary Government in Colonies. London: Hansard Society, 1953.

The Future of the House of Lords. London: Hansard Society. New York: Praeger, 1954.

PAMPHLETS

United Europe. London: National News-Letter. Second edition, 1948.

The Palace of Westminster. London: Hansard Society, 1949.

Constitutions of British Colonies. London: Hansard Society, 1950.

The Korean Crisis. London: National Peace Council, 1950.

Lords and Commons. London: H.M. Stationery Office, 1951.

Parliamentary Government. London: British Council, second edition, 1958.

The Troika and the Future of the U.N. New York: Carnegie Endowment for International Peace, 1962.

Sydney D. Bailey

THE SECRETARIAT OF THE UNITED NATIONS

Revised Edition

Published under the auspices of the
Carnegie Endowment for International Peace

FREDERICK A. PRAEGER, *Publishers*
New York • Washington • London

FREDERICK A. PRAEGER, *Publishers*
111 Fourth Avenue, New York 3, N.Y., U.S.A.
77-79 Charlotte Street, London W.1, England

Revised edition published in the United States of America in 1964
by Frederick A. Praeger, Inc., Publishers

The original clothbound edition of this book was published
in 1962 by Carnegie Endowment for International Peace, New York

Library of Congress Catalog Card Number: 64-22486

Printed in the United States of America

CONTENTS

CONTENTS

CHARTS AND TABLES

PREFACE

IN the introduction to his annual report in 1962, U Thant wrote of a 'crisis of confidence' through which the United Nations was passing, but he added that he had faith that the Organization would survive the 'crisis' and emerge stronger than before. A year later, he felt able to report 'without being charged with undue optimism' that the 'crisis' had largely disappeared.[*1]

It is natural that we should associate the United Nations with crises. Indeed, one of the main purposes of the Organization is to deal with disputes and difficulties which threaten world peace. But the crisis of confidence of which U Thant wrote did not arise solely from the fact that the United Nations was being asked to deal with such matters; the crisis was also a reflection of differences of view among Member States, including some of the founder Members, about the meaning and implications of the Charter. To what extent do the obligations of the Charter limit the freedom of action of the sovereign Member States? In what circumstances, and by what means, should the United Nations act when it is claimed that world peace is threatened? Is the Secretary-General empowered to take independent initiatives which, in his view, accord with the principles and advance the purposes of the Charter?

It was natural that during this period of questioning, considerable attention should be paid to the machinery of the United Nations: the possibility of amending the Charter, particularly to provide for the enlargement of the Security

* The references, which are numbered consecutively, will be found on pages 117-26.

Council and the Economic and Social Council; the Organization's financial problems, which had arisen because of disagreement as to whether Members of the United Nations do or do not have collective financial responsibility for peace-keeping operations; the procedure and methods of work of the General Assembly and other organs; the composition and responsibilities of the Secretariat.

The Secretariat is one of the principal organs of the United Nations. It is to serve all the Members, and yet remain independent of them. The responsibilities of the Secretary-General and staff are, as the Charter puts it, 'exclusively international'. There have, to be sure, been occasional lapses from the high standards of the Charter, in this as in other respects. One should, therefore, ask whether the provisions of the Charter regarding the Secretariat are adequate for the needs of the United Nations as it has developed since 1945. Have difficulties occurred because the Charter has not been properly implemented or because the Charter is now out of date?

These are the questions I seek to discuss in this book. I begin by examining the general constitutional framework within which the Secretariat operates. In chapter 2 I am concerned with the evolution of the concept of an independent and international civil service. I then pass to the responsibilities entrusted to the Secretary-General; in particular, I consider some of the implications of the *troika* and similar proposals. In the final chapter I deal with a number of organizational matters, including problems which have arisen regarding recruitment of staff.

During the course of writing the book, I was able to consult a number of members and former members of the Secretariat and of national delegations to the United Nations. I am grateful to those, necessarily anonymous, who helped me in this way.

Sydney D. Bailey

January 1964

THE SECRETARIAT OF THE UNITED NATIONS

I

THE UNITED NATIONS: RETROSPECT AND PROSPECT

THE minimum foreign policy of a nation—any nation—was, by implication, written into the United Nations Charter. It is to preserve the territorial integrity and political independence of the State. Boundaries of States may be unjust, governments may be tyrannical, but the Charter prohibits the threat or use of force in international relations to put things right. The Charter does not explicitly forbid interference by one State in the domestic political affairs of another State; it does not exclude territorial revision. What it does is to oblige all Members of the Organization to refrain from threatening or using force in such matters. Injustices are to be remedied by peaceful means and in such a manner that international peace and security and justice are not endangered.

There are only two exceptions to the ban on force in international relations. First, if an armed attack occurs against a Member of the United Nations, States may exercise the inherent right of individual or collective self-defence until the Security Council has taken measures necessary to maintain international peace and security. Secondly, if peace is threatened or breached or aggression occurs, the Security Council may authorize the use of force as a last resort. The chief purpose of the United Nations is thus to prevent the unilateral exercise of force, except in self-defence, even in the face of extreme and persistent provocation, and to ensure that if aggression does occur, it is resisted by the united strength of all Members.

These are far-reaching commitments, and to discharge them Members have, by the Charter, conferred primary responsibility for maintaining international peace and security on the Security Council. Members have agreed that the Council acts on their behalf. They have undertaken to accept the Council's decisions, and to afford mutual assistance in carrying out all measures decided upon by the Council. Moreover, the primacy of the Security Council was safeguarded by restrictions in the Charter on the role of the General Assembly in maintaining peace.[2]

The responsibility conferred on the Security Council is, however, 'primary'; it is not exclusive. The International Court of Justice has emphasized that 'the General Assembly is also to be concerned with international peace and security', although 'only the Security Council . . . can require enforcement by coercive action against an aggressor'.[3]

Decisions of the Security Council on substantive questions are possible only when the permanent members are in agreement—or, at any rate, when they are willing to refrain from exercising the veto. But if an armed attack occurs and the Security Council is prevented by the veto from taking measures to maintain international peace and security, the right of self-defence is unimpaired.

The Charter: Theory and Practice

To describe the first purpose of the United Nations as I have done is to refer to a world which exists only in the Charter. States may love peace, but they sometimes love other things more. States may be able to carry out the obligations of the Charter, but they are not always willing to do so. And although the Charter does not regard failure by one Member to honour its obligations as a reason why other Members should be released from the same or some other obligation, in practice the *tu quoque* argument has always been popular.

There are other purposes of the United Nations besides the main one of dealing with threats to the peace and acts of aggression. These purposes, as specified in the Charter, are: to bring about by peaceful means the adjustment of international disputes or situations; to develop friendly relations among nations; to achieve international cooperation in non-political matters; and to be a center for harmonizing the actions of nations. But if the Charter is considered as a whole, it is clear that these purposes, though unquestionably important, were intended to be subsidiary.

The Charter is a product of the pre-nuclear age. The anarchy of unilateral State action was to be replaced by a limited system of international order. States were in theory declared to be sovereign, but in practice their sovereignty was to be restricted to the extent that the Security Council could reach a decision. Experience had shown that a nation could survive an aggressive onslaught and win. The idea in 1945 was that the international community would come to the aid of victims of aggression, but it seems not to have been envisaged that there might be no survivors to be assisted.

The awful nature of contemporary weapons makes necessary a more radical plan for world order than is contained in the Charter. Such a plan would no doubt include a program of universal disarmament, to be carried out by stages and with effective control; the strengthening of the rule of law; the development of improved machinery for creating and transporting an international police force when required; and better measures for resolving international disputes by peaceful means. The McCloy-Zorin agreement on disarmament in 1961 committed the two major powers to most of these goals in principle. A viable system of international order may well demand some ultimate revision of the United Nations Charter, further limiting the freedom of action of States, but this depends on great power unanimity; the immediate task is to ensure than the Charter we have is honoured.

The present Charter does not embody perfection. Some of its provisions are contradictory, some are imprecise, some are easier to formulate than to implement, and some important eventualities were not provided for. But when the criticisms have been made, the fact remains that the Charter does provide a basis for international cooperation, with sufficient flexibility that adjustments of practice can be made (and have been made) in the light of changing circumstances. If, in this study, I accord to the Charter what may seem an undue degree of respect, it is not because I consider that there is no scope for improving it. The Charter is an international treaty, binding on all States which choose to accept the obligations of membership. All Members of the United Nations have agreed that, in the event of a conflict between the obligations of the Charter and other obligations, the Charter prevails. In a world in which States pursue what they conceive to be the national interest but in which to do so is unprecedentedly risky, a limited system of international order is essential and can be achieved only by an Organization which seeks to act in the larger interests of mankind. The Charter is a fundamental law not only for Members of the Organization but also for the Secretary-General and the staff.

It has been said that the Charter and the Organization it establishes are based on Western principles and ideas, and that many States in the modern world are not content that their affairs should be ordered according to principles and ideas which evolved in the West for the protection and preservation of selfish Western interests. In particular, it has been said that the Charter tends to freeze the *status quo* and inhibit change, whereas what is needed is a dynamic system of international relations that fosters such desirable changes as the elimination of colonialism and the economic and social advancement of the less-developed parts of the world.

That ideas and principles contained in the Charter originated in a particular part of the world should be a reason neither for accepting nor for rejecting them; the test should be whether they accord with that elusive thing, the general interest. We should not cling to principles simply because they are familiar, but equally we should not discard them because we disapprove of certain acts of those who invented them.

The idea of a world organization to keep the peace is relatively novel. Nobody had given much thought to it before the seventeenth century, and the nations of the world have been able to use a general international organization as an element of foreign policy only for about forty years at most, and for the majority of nations for very much less. There are obvious reasons why men think of the United Nations in terms that are familiar in national political life. The General Assembly and the Councils are like legislatures; the International Court is a judiciary; the Secretariat is analogous to a civil service. Expressions drawn from domestic politics, and the ideas underlying the expressions, are freely used. The term 'parliamentary diplomacy' has been coined by Dean Rusk to describe the operations of such organs as the General Assembly. An agenda is drawn up, items are debated, motions are introduced, votes are taken. The doctrine of sovereign equality, of one State having one vote, is said to be 'democratic'. It all looks rather like the sort of thing that takes place in national capitals.

The differences, however, are significant. There is the difference in public attitude, the fact that few people feel the same sort of allegiance to the United Nations as they do to their own countries. There are also institutional differences. In the United Nations system there are several 'legislatures', not one, and there is no 'government', no cohesive and continuous focus of political leadership that submits proposals to the legislative organs, and controls and coordinates the activities of the civil service. One consequence of this absence of a 'government' has been that the United Nations has experimented with various ways of ordering its affairs within the broad framework of the Charter. The underlying purpose of these experiments has, in essence, been to discover a workable means of decision-making in the international interest.

Security Council and General Assembly

The founders of the United Nations intended to give the Big Five a paramount role in questions relating to world peace. The Security Council was accorded primary responsibility for maintaining international peace and security, and the Big Five were to have permanent membership of the Council, with the right of veto in virtually all non-procedural matters. The position of primacy of the Security Council, and within the Council of its five permanent members, was hardly compatible with the principle that all the Members of the Organization are sovereign and equal. If States were really equal, all or none would have the veto. The fact is that the medium and smaller States at San Francisco were ambivalent in their attitude to the Big Five. On the one hand, they believed that real peace in the post-war world would be unattainable in the absence of great power unity. On the other hand, they feared that if the great powers were too united, their own legitimate interests would be ignored.

In the event, neither the hopes nor the fears that were apparent at San Francisco have been fully realized. The interests of the great powers have no doubt coincided more often than the record of voting in United Nations organs would suggest. All the same, the cold war has caused or complicated most international questions since 1945.

A divided world is from almost every point of view regrettable; it has been the cause of suffering and bloodshed,

6

and its indefinite continuance could lead not merely to hot war but to the extinction of humanity. But at least it can be said that the United Nations has not been an instrument for the domination of the world by the great powers. Indeed, the Organization has increasingly become the forum, the helper, even the protector, of the smaller powers.

Be that as it may, the Security Council has not discharged the functions assigned to it in the Charter. The veto was embodied in the Charter because it seemed inconceivable that the Organization would ever attempt to coerce one of the great powers. Since all States could be bound by the decisions of the Security Council (though only eleven would be actual members at any one time), the veto was a procedural mechanism which would prevent rank-and-file Members of the Organization from being compelled to engage in coercive action against one of the great powers.

But in practice the veto has been used for quite other purposes—for example, to block the admission of States to membership in the United Nations and to prevent the Security Council from calling upon the parties to a dispute to seek a solution by peaceful means.

If the veto were used capriciously, one of two consequences would follow. Either means would be sought to circumvent it, or the Organization would lapse into futility. The widespread wish of Member States to obtain some limitation of the exercise of the veto, and the support for such circumventing devices as the 'Uniting for Peace' procedure, make it clear that governments have not wished the United Nations to sink into futility.

The limited effectiveness of the Security Council in the face of great power disunity led to efforts, partially successful, to strengthen the General Assembly's role regarding the maintenance of peace and security. In 1947, an attempt was made to establish the General Assembly on a continuous basis by the creation of the Interim Committee (the Little Assembly), and in 1950 the General Assembly adopted the 'Uniting for Peace' resolution which included provisions for transferring responsibility to the General Assembly when the Security Council was deadlocked by the veto. The General Assembly has been called into emergency special session to deal with four questions under the 'Uniting for Peace' procedure: Hungary in 1956, Suez in 1956, Lebanon and Jordan in 1958, and the Congo in 1960.

Procedures of this kind do not, of themselves, change the essential character of the conflicts; they merely affect the forums in which they are examined. The power realities that had made the veto seem necessary still exist. The cold war is not eliminated by changing the organ in which it is debated; differences of ideology and purpose remain.

It is sometimes suggested that the Assembly is hampered because its decisions do not have binding force, but this is not wholly correct. In certain matters the Assembly has full authority to take binding decisions. It has exclusive responsibility for electing members of the three Councils; it approves the budget of the Organization and apportions the expenses among Members; it approves any financial or budgetary arrangements with specialized agencies; it establishes regulations for the appointment of staff. The General Assembly also acts with the Security Council regarding the admission, suspension, or expulsion of Members, the appointment of the Secretary-General, and amendments to the Charter. In these matters, Members of the United Nations are under an obligation to respect in good faith the decisions of the General Assembly. But in other matters regarding the maintenance of international peace and security, whether under the 'Uniting for Peace' or any other procedure, decisions of the General Assembly are recommendations or expressions of opinion.

Dag Hammarskjold took the view that recommendations of the General Assembly may tend more and more to be recognized as having weight and binding effect, particularly when they involve the application of the principles of the Charter and of international law. He held that if the Organization were to grow into an increasingly effective instrument, this would be because Members not only accepted fully the Charter obligation to carry out the decisions of the Security Council, but also accorded increasing respect to the recommendations of the Assembly.[4]

The Security Council was intended to mirror the power realities that existed when the United Nations was created, whereas the General Assembly was to reflect another aspect of the state of international relations, that which is based on the principle of the sovereign equality of all Members of the Organization. Many people in the newly independent States of Asia, the Middle East, and Africa have had little patience with the ideological and political belligerency that has characterized the cold war and frustrated the effective working of the Security Council. The leaders of the new States are, in the main, interested in other things. They wish to remain free of entanglements with either camp and have looked to the United Nations for the protection which was traditionally sought in alliances. During the past decade, the work of the General Assembly has been increasingly permeated by a mood of non-alignment, a reluctance to take sides in quarrels between the major powers, a hope of achieving security through non-commitment.

The General Assembly can be a somewhat volatile organ. Its size, the fluctuating interests of its Members, the methods of conducting its business, and a preoccupation on the part of the representatives of some Member States with the more dramatic manifestations of parliamentary diplomacy—these have constituted serious, though not insuperable, obstacles in the way of prompt and decisive action when peace was threatened or breached. Moreover, some Member States have had reservations about the legal propriety or political expediency of those decisions of the General Assembly which, in

9

substance even if not in form, sought to go beyond the making of recommendations.

When it has been impossible to muster sufficient votes in the Security Council or the General Assembly for any proposal of substance, Members have usually been content either to avoid substantive decisions by such respectable diplomatic devices as postponement, or to transfer the responsibility for action to the Secretary-General by declaring in broad terms the objectives to be achieved. Most governments have been glad to turn to the Secretary-General when other methods would not work. In fulfilling the tasks entrusted to them in this way, the Secretaries-General have had significant advantages: the high prestige attaching to the Office deriving from its constitutional independence; their own personal integrity, courage, tact, and skill; and the respect which Members of the Organization have normally accorded to them. All the same, difficulties were bound to arise if policy-making organs indicated general objectives but without giving guidance as to the means to be employed, and if Member States failed to make available the resources of men and money necessary to implement established policy. Moreover, the problem has not been only that the Secretaries-General have not always received sufficient guidance or resources; some of the most difficult problems were not foreseen, and could not have been foreseen, when the original mandate was conferred.

Purposes of a World Organization

The United Nations might be regarded as representing a stage in the evolution of international society, with some form of world government as the eventual goal. Alternatively, the United Nations might be thought of as the goal itself, making possible the maximum amount of international collaboration that States will accept. For it is by no means self-evident that world government is a desirable aim. Probably most people feel instinctively, with Emerson, that the less government we have the better—national government or world government. And for the orthodox communist there are particular difficulties about world government arising partly from the Marxist belief that the state will wither away, and partly also from tactical considerations regarding cooperation with bourgeois regimes until the goal of universal communism is achieved. All the same, communists are realists and the Russian leaders have in recent years modified their views on such matters as the inevitability of war with capitalist States. This modification followed a realistic assessment of the character of modern weapons and the likely consequences of an all-out nuclear war. A Soviet re-examination of the nature and purposes of a general international organization to keep the peace should not be excluded. The United Nations, even if it does no more than provide a forum for the confrontation of differing views, serves a purpose which few States can afford to neglect.

But is it enough to have a United Nations merely to provide a place for international conferences, an arena where international differences can be conveniently discussed? This is by no means a negligible role, since any organization that facilitates contacts and understanding across barriers is important. It is not, therefore, to belittle this function to suggest that the United Nations has other and more important tasks to perform.

The poorer countries (and most countries are poorer) look to the United Nations and the related agencies for help in their economic and social advancement. Assistance from multilateral sources avoids some of the political embarrassments of bilateral arrangements. United Nations development programs may be marginal in scale when contrasted with some national or regional programs, but United Nations aid is increasing in quantity and effectiveness, and for some countries provides the only hope that rising expectations can be satisfied.

I doubt, however, whether an effective future for the United Nations in the economic and social field can be ensured unless the Organization is also achieving some success in political and security matters. It is perhaps theoretically conceivable that the United Nations could continue to promote economic and social cooperation even though its political institutions were wholly or relatively ineffective. To some extent this was true of the League of Nations; the International Labour Organization, in particular, continued to play an important role in a limited field even after the League itself had begun to decline. But if the United Nations were manifestly to fail in its primary political functions, the more developed countries would probably choose to divert an increasing amount of assistance to the less fortunate areas through channels that might be less acceptable to the recipients.

It is true that there are many things which, in present conditions of international society, the United Nations cannot do. It cannot exercise direct physical coercion against the most powerful States. It can make moral appeals; it can regret or condemn; but it cannot take collective enforcement measures against a permanent member of the Security Council. Great power aggression must be deterred or resisted by other means, or tolerated.

There are, however, many threats to international peace that do not arise from the direct confrontation of the major powers. Local territorial disputes, friction arising from resistance to or absence of decolonization, revolution and counter-revolution, liberation and counter-liberation, discontent on the part of minorities, secessionist risings, acute political instability, infiltration and subversion—these may occur at points geographically remote from the major powers and yet in a way that threatens to embroil them. In a number of cases of this kind, the United Nations has sought to insulate the problem from direct great power involvement by inserting the physical presence of the Organization's representatives at the actual seat of difficulty. One may criticize particular aspects of particular United Nations operations or complain that United Nations organs have not followed a consistent standard in discharging their peace-keeping functions, and yet recognize that the Organization has in a number of critical situations exerted a tranquillizing influence and minimized, halted, or prevented intervention from outside while passions cooled.

A great danger at the present time is war by accident, misunderstanding, or miscalculation. The problem is in part a technical one, and a partial solution must be sought in measures of disarmament or arms control, whether by international agreement or unilateral initiative. An equal threat arises from the possibility that the great powers could be drawn into taking sides in some local conflict, not because of any direct or immediate interest but to forestall intervention by others. There can be no guarantee that wars of liberation can be limited. There are, after all, forms of indirect intervention, such as the use of 'volunteers', which may provoke counter-intervention of a direct nature.

The United Nations can insulate and limit local difficulties, but it can do this effectively only if the policy-making bodies consistently seek to discharge their responsibilities in accordance with the principles of the Charter. Moreover, if the United Nations is to play more than a conference role, the Secretariat must be enabled to act promptly and impartially in implementing the decisions of the policy-making bodies. The staff must be preserved from political pressures, not only because the Charter says so, but also because a Secretariat composed of persons seeking to represent national views and promote national policies could rapidly bring the United Nations to a chaotic standstill. Governmental positions are legitimately expressed in speeches and votes in policy-making organs; once decisions have been reached, it is for the Secretariat to accept and carry them out.

These conclusions, stated rather baldly in this introductory chapter, necessarily leave out of account a great many difficulties. How should the Secretariat act if decisions of the policy-making bodies are vague, ambiguous, or contradictory? What should the Secretariat do if problems arise which were not foreseen when the original decision was reached? Is the notion of an independent civil service understood and accepted in enough countries for it to be worth pursuing in the United Nations? Should an international official seek to divorce himself completely from national origins? These are some of the questions I examine in the light of the historical evolution of the machinery of international organization, of present legal obligations, and of the concrete needs of international politics at this time.

2

AN INTERNATIONAL CIVIL SERVICE: THE GROWTH OF AN IDEA

THE civil service as a social institution can be traced into a far distant past. One of the oldest and most distinguished was that created by the Chinese. On the European continent, the forerunner of the modern civil service was the powerful and able service of the Romans which disintegrated under the impact of feudalism. For several centuries thereafter, professional civil services consisted of the personal household staff of hereditary monarchs and feudal lords. No distinction was made between policy and administration, and the idea of the separation of powers was unknown.

The modern concept of an impersonal civil service began to emerge in the West during the seventeenth century, and came to fruition during the nineteenth century. The size of units of government was growing, partly as a consequence of outlying territories being brought under central administration; increasingly independent civil services provided an element of unity in situations of cultural and territorial diversity. The rise of democratic ideas, with changes of government depending to a greater or lesser extent on public opinion, made necessary an element of administrative continuity—a civil service independent of political changes.

It is true that many problems encountered in international relations are unique: we cannot assume that institutions that have evolved in national politics will have any necessary relevance to international affairs. All the same, the two needs which in national societies led to the emergence of independent civil services exist today in the relations between nations: the need for unity, as diverse nations seek to harmonize their actions in the attainment of common ends; and the need for administrative continuity, independent of the shifting interests and allegiances of States.

It seems that the first discussion of the idea of an international secretariat is in William Penn's essay on an international parliament, first published in 1693. It is significant that Penn chose as his model the one professional group which, throughout a turbulent century, had demonstrated an unusual capacity for impartiality and independence.

Penn had proposed the establishment of an assembly of nations before which could be brought disputes that had not been settled by conventional diplomacy, and the decisions of which would be enforced by collective action. Penn's proposed secretariat was based on the arrangements of the English House of Commons. Officials, called 'clerks', were to be appointed, one for every ten representatives in the assembly. The clerks were to sit at a 'pew or table' in the assembly hall, receive written complaints, and keep the journals of proceedings. At the end of each session, a select committee of representatives would examine and compare the journals. The journals would then be stored in a chest with several locks, each clerk having one key. States would be entitled to have copies of the journals and all communications received by the secretariat.

For more than two centuries, Penn's idea lay dormant. Indeed, when proposals for the League of Nations were first under discussion, attention was directed almost exclusively to the powers and procedures of the deliberative organs.

Neither the Phillimore Plan nor Colonel House's draft covenant contained any reference to administrative machinery. General Smuts included in his plan a brief reference to a secretariat, and all important proposals thereafter maintained at least the bare idea of permanent administrative machinery.

League Experience

Probably because so little advance thought had been given to the matter, and also because there were no exact predecents, the Covenant of the League said little about administrative matters.* The Secretariat was to be a permanent institution, established at the seat of the League, and was to comprise a Secretary-General and such secretaries and staff as might be required. The first Secretary-General was to be the person named in the Annex to the Covenant (Sir Eric Drummond), and his successors were to be appointed by the Council with the approval of the majority of the Assembly. The secretaries and staff were to be appointed by the Secretary-General with the approval of the Council; all positions in the Secretariat were to be open equally to men and women. The Secretary-General was to 'act in that capacity at all meetings of the Assembly and of the Council'.[5]

It was left to Drummond to add flesh to this skeleton. Earlier intergovernmental agencies had been staffed either by nationals of the host country or by officials seconded by governments. Drummond dreamed of an international career service based on merit alone, though it was never possible wholly to achieve this ideal. From the start, there was pressure to allocate some posts on the basis of nationality. Fluent use of one of the two official languages—English and French —was regarded as an essential qualification. Financial stringency hindered the recruiting of staff from countries distant from Geneva.

There were other difficulties, too. The League was

* See Appendix A, page 101.

17

regarded in some quarters as a bold and risky adventure; a career in the Secretariat could hardly offer an official the security he would have expected in his own civil service. Devotion to the ideals of the League did not, of itself, constitute a sufficient qualification, nor did it necessarily contribute to a team spirit. Separation from national ways of life is the lot of all who live abroad, but the international official must adjust not only to the traditions and habits of the country in which he resides, but also to the varied traditions and habits of his colleagues in the international secretariat.

Drummond was by nature cautious and self-effacing. He was by training a British civil servant—anonymous, remote, impartial. His role in the life of the League was a creative one, but almost always behind the scenes. He considered that the Secretariat should prepare the ground for and implement the decisions of the Council and the Assembly, but should not itself decide questions of policy. He believed that the Secretariat should be international in two senses: international in its composition, and international in its responsibilities.

These ideals were always difficult to maintain, but particularly so after fascist and nazi ideas began to gain ground. A stage was eventually reached when some senior officials in the Secretariat considered themselves to be national representatives.

A former League official has commented:

> We were finally not even allowed to write directly to Italian members on our technical committees without passing through the Italian Undersecretary-General's office with the Secretariat; he then passed the letter to the Foreign Office in Rome before it finally reached its destination.[6]

As early as 1930 this trend found expression in the minority report signed by the German and Italian members of the Committee of Thirteen, which was appointed to review the administration of the League Secretariat, the International Labour Office, and the Registry of the Court.[7]

Count Bernstorff and M. Gallavresi pointed out that the League Secretariat had been growing in size and importance. The political character of the Secretariat's work had been accentuated, and the execution of decisions taken by organs of the League constantly required interpretations and judgments of a political nature.

> So long as there is no Super-State, and therefore no 'international man', an international spirit can only be assured through the cooperation of men of different nationalities who represent the public opinion of their respective countries.

There was, they maintained, no real sharing of responsibility among senior officials; the meeting of Directors held nearly every week did not engage in discussion of delicate matters. Two possible remedies were suggested. A system of joint control by a limited number of high officials could be established. This collective executive body would

> discuss in plenary session all general questions, of any kind whatever, and . . . would consider the action to be taken in pursuance of the decisions of the Council and the Assembly, would take steps to ensure liaison with States Members, examine the draft agendas of the Assembly, Council and Committees, study the documents submitted to the Assembly, Council and Committees, authorize officials to proceed on missions, and examine the reports submitted by these officials to the Secretariat on the completion of their missions in the different countries.

A less far-reaching possibility would be to appoint a small committee of under-secretaries-general to assist and advise the Secretary-General. This committee would have the right to give its opinion before any measures involving important political issues or principles were taken by the Secretary-General. The committee would replace the Secretary-General in the general control of affairs if for any reason he were absent from duty, thus, it was said, ensuring the international character of the Secretariat.[8]

The issues raised by Bernstorff and Gallavresi were not simply administrative in character. If the League were thought of merely as a piece of conference machinery, their ideas might have had some validity. But the fact was that the League had an existence independent of its constituent elements; it possessed international personality and legal capacity. The Covenant had referred to 'the League' as something different from the sum of its members, and 'the League' had in practice assumed functions which required that the Secretariat should be loyal to the League as an entity and not simply be a mirror of national viewpoints. The Bernstorff-Gallavresi proposals were rejected.

United Nations Secretariat

The founders of the United Nations intended to embody in the Charter those improvements which seemed necessary in the light of the experience of the League and the International Labour Organization. The Secretariat is declared to be one of the six 'principal organs' of the United Nations and is to consist of a Secretary-General and staff appointed by him.* The procedure for appointing the Secretary-General was adapted from the procedure of the League; but, whereas appointments to the League staff required the formal approval of the Council, the Secretary-General of the United Nations was given sole authority to appoint staff, subject only to 'regulations' to be established by the General Assembly.

The Secretary-General was described as 'the chief

* The relevant Articles of the Charter are reproduced in Appendix B, pages 102–3.

administrative officer of the Organization'. He was to 'act in that capacity' in all meetings of the General Assembly and the three Councils; to assign staff from the Secretariat to the various organs as required; to perform such functions as might be entrusted to him by the General Assembly and the Councils; and to report annually to the General Assembly on the work of the Organization.

Article 99 of the Charter represented a new departure. This Article empowers the Secretary-General to 'bring to the attention of the Security Council any matter which in his opinion may threaten the maintenance of international peace and security', whereas the League Covenant had merely provided that in the event of war or threat of war, the Secretary-General should 'on the request of any Member of the League' summon a meeting of the Council.[9] Britain proposed at Dumbarton Oaks that the head of the United Nations Secretariat should have the right, on his own initiative and without the request of a Member State, to draw the attention of the Council (later called the Security Council) to any dispute or situation which he thought might endanger world peace and security. This was approved at Dumbarton Oaks and later at San Francisco. Article 99 does not, of course, derogate from the functions and powers of the Security Council; the purpose is to ensure that the Security Council shall have the opportunity of considering a matter within its competence, even if no State takes the formal step of requesting such consideration.

The requirements of the Charter regarding the independence of the Secretariat (Article 100) were adapted from Article 1 of the Staff Regulations of the League. The provisions relating to criteria for recruiting staff, contained in Article 101 (3), were based on proposals made by New Zealand and Canada at San Francisco. The Soviet and Ukrainian Delegations proposed the omission of these criteria on the ground that technical details should be omitted from the Charter, but the text was approved by 26 votes to 6.[10]

Articles 100 and 101 of the Charter constitute a legal basis for the independence, integrity, and impartiality required of the staff. The oath or declaration of office, approved by the General Assembly, and subscribed to by all members of the staff, makes the obligations more explicit.

> I solemnly swear (undertake, affirm, promise) to exercise in all loyalty, discretion and conscience the functions entrusted to me as an international civil servant of the United Nations, to discharge these functions and regulate my conduct with the interests of the United Nations only in view, and not to seek or accept instructions in regard to the performance of my duties from any government or other authority external to the Organization.[11]

The intentions of the Charter and the oath or declaration of office are clear. Officials of the United Nations are not expected to give up their beliefs, but they are not national representatives; they are international officials and are expected to act only in the interests of the Organization.

The responsibilities of the Secretariat derive from the Charter, the Staff Regulations established by the General Assembly, the rules of procedure of the organs of the United Nations, and the decisions of these organs in particular cases. The magnitude of the responsibilities of the Secretariat has tended to increase, in part because of the need to develop better institutions for international cooperation, in part simply because of the passage of time. The international aspects of problems arising from the development of atomic energy and the exploration of outer space, for example, are matters of concern to the United Nations. Organs are created to deal with these questions, and the organs must be served by qualified personnel. But the assumption of such new responsibilities does not mean that old ones can be neglected. The United Nations is still concerned with the regulation of conventional armaments and with international cooperation regarding conventional sources of energy. Again, the fact that the United Nations took on heavy responsibilities in the Congo did not eliminate its responsibilities in Kashmir or Korea. The eruption of a crisis in Angola does not lessen concern regarding *apartheid*.

Moreover, the increase in the responsibilities of the Secretariat has not been confined to the political field; there has also been a remarkable expansion of economic and social programs. Originally, the main task of the Secretariat in economic and social affairs was to service the policy-making organs. At an early stage, however, the Secretariat was asked to make studies and undertake research. By 1950 it had been given responsibilities for substantive field operations, and these operations have increased in extent and in importance. Only in relation to dependent territories is there likely to be a contraction in the responsibilities of the United Nations. This has been accompanied by a doubling of the Organization's membership, necessitating increased services in other areas.

The extension of the responsibilities of the Secretariat was not the result of preconceived notions; it was not an improper usurpation of authority by the bureaucracy. It was made necessary by the facts of international life and was authorized by the appropriate organs of the United Nations. The consequence, however, has been to enhance rather than reduce the importance of the ideals of the Charter regarding the character of the Secretariat.

In appointing the staff, as in all his duties, the Secretary-General should neither seek nor receive instructions from any government or authority external to the United Nations, and he should appoint only those who will neither seek nor receive such instructions. For purely practical reasons, the Secretaries-General have been glad to have the help of governments regarding appointments. Secretary-General Lie made it clear that, while reserving to himself the final decision on the basis of all the facts, he had sought the assistance of governments in checking the character and records of applicants and staff members. The United Nations, he held, did not and clearly could not have the facilities for personnel selection which are at the disposal of national governments. The assistance of governments in providing facts seemed to him essential and did not derogate from his exclusive authority.[12]

This practice had its origin in the difficulty of screening applicants and staff in the initial period of intensive recruitment. By formal or informal consultations with governments, it was often possible to obtain a list of candidates and to check the factual information supplied by applicants or staff members. Some governments went further and offered opinions about the suitability of particular persons for employment as international officials. But such consultation does not give governments any rights regarding appointments, nor does it detract from the exclusive responsibility of the Secretary-General regarding the appointment of staff.

Indeed, the Preparatory Commission specifically rejected a proposal that staff appointments should have the concurrence of the governments of the candidates concerned. It had been suggested by one delegation that governments were often in the best position to assess the qualifications and capacities of prospective staff members, but a large number of delegations opposed the proposal. They argued that it would impinge upon the exclusive responsibility of the Secretary-General under Article 101 of the Charter and threaten the freedom, independence, and truly international character of the Secretariat. They maintained that although the staff should as far as possible be acceptable to governments, it would be extremely undesirable to give national governments particular rights in this respect or to permit political pressure on the Secretary-General. Moreover, they doubted whether national governments were always well qualified to pronounce upon the suitability of candidates. The proposal was defeated by 'a large majority'.[13] Nevertheless, the idea that all persons appointed to the staff should be sponsored by governments still persists in some quarters.[14]

Before 1960, the main challenge to the principles embodied in Articles 100 and 101 of the Charter had been particular rather than general. Governments or other public authorities had, in a number of cases, sought special rights in relation to their own nationals. Governments had occasionally complained that some of their nationals in the Secretariat were unsuitable for continued employment as international officials because they had been recruited at a time when a different regime was in power at home.[15] The Secretaries-General have resisted such pressures because the capacity of an official to serve the United Nations should be independent of changes in the character of authorities external to the Organization. Staff members have, indeed, continued to serve the United Nations with undiminished dedication after there have been changes of government, *coups d'état*, or revolutions at home.[16]

The most overt threat to the principles of Articles 100 and 101, to which Hammarskjold referred in his speech at Oxford University on 20 May 1961, had come at the height of the McCarthy era.[17] Charges had been made in the United States that an unspecified number of US citizens employed in the Secretariat had engaged in subversive activities, and a Federal Grand Jury and the Internal Security Subcommittee of the Senate Judiciary Committee conducted investigations into these allegations. A number of US citizens in the Secretariat, invoking their constitutional privilege, refused to answer certain questions, and this inflamed some sections of American opinion against the United Nations. Secretary-General Lie made it clear that no one should serve in the Secretariat if there was substantial evidence indicating subversive activities directed against his own or any other State, but it was widely felt that any United Nations decisions regarding allegations of disloyalty or subversion should be based on its own investigations and evaluations. The General Assembly, having received Lie's report on the matter, expressed its confidence that the Secretary-General would conduct personnel policy with the provisions of the Charter in mind.[18] All the same, the adoption of this bland resolution did not conceal the anxiety, within the Secretariat and elsewhere, concerning the implications of public national investigations of international officials, even making allowance for any special rights of the host country.

No Secretary-General would knowingly appoint a person who had engaged in acts of subversion against any State; but the commission of subversive acts is a very different thing from mere disagreement with the policy of a particular government. Any conscientious official of the United Nations is likely, at some time or another, to have questioned or disapproved of a particular act or policy of his own government, but this should not interfere with his loyalty toward the Organization he is obligated to serve.

Sometimes there has been pressure on the Secretary-General to go beyond the requirements of Article 101(3) and, in appointing or promoting staff, to give favoured treatment to persons solely or mainly on grounds of nationality. It is no secret that some governments have sought to influence personnel policy in this way, perhaps in the belief that their interests will in some way be promoted if their own nationals occupy important positions in the Secretariat. There can be no justification for the view, which has sometimes been expressed in United Nations meetings, that countries or regions with a relatively large number of nationals in the Secretariat are by this means able to exert an improper influence on the Organization.[19] If staff members conduct themselves as required by the Charter, there can be no question of any state as such having any direct influence through its citizens in the Secretariat. It is legitimate to complain to the Secretary-General that particular staff members have failed to honour their obligation as international officials, but the mere fact of numbers is not evidence of improper influence.

I am not, of course, asserting that a wide geographical basis for the recruitment of staff is not desirable. An international organization should be staffed on an international basis. Pressure to achieve still wider geographical distribution in the Secretariat is proper, but it should be exerted in a way that does not reflect on the character or performance of existing staff members.

International Loyalty

Much of the discussion of international loyalty tends to be somewhat glib. The concept is a subtle one, not easily defined. Its key elements are stated in the Staff Regulations to be integrity, independence, and impartiality.[20]

Integrity is a matter of personal ethics, without any necessary connection with national origin, religious conviction or political viewpoint. It comprises such elementary qualities as honesty, truthfulness, fidelity, probity, and freedom from corrupting influences, but the International Civil Service Advisory Board has emphasized that the Charter requires integrity as a public official, and especially as an international public official, and this involves the subordination of private interests where those interests would conflict with the interests of the Organization.[21] Moreover, integrity includes the idea of complete and consistent discretion. An international official should not, either during or after his employment in the Secretariat, communicate to any person any confidential information acquired in the course of his duties, unless authorized to do so by the Secretary-General.[22]

Independence, in the context of Articles 100 and 105 of the Charter, means that an international official should be impervious to external pressure or influence. He enjoys such privileges and immunities as are necessary for the independent discharge of his responsibilities, and he should take no orders

from his own or any other government during his period of
service with the United Nations.

Impartiality is the third requirement. The classic concept of state neutrality concerned actions and not convictions,
and this kind of neutrality may reasonably be asked of members of the Secretariat. Any normal human being has beliefs,
and a member of the Secretariat is not expected to give these
up.

> However, his expression of these beliefs, his actions, any
> public pronouncements he makes, his general conduct—
> all must be consonant with his international status, and
> must conform to the interests of the United Nations to
> which his service is dedicated.[23]
>
> Members of the Secretariat . . . are not expected to give
> up their national sentiments or their political and religious
> convictions, [but] they shall at all times bear in mind the
> reserve and tact incumbent upon them by reason of their
> international status.[24]

The Secretaries-General have rightly distinguished between
beliefs and actions. 'I am not neutral as regards the Charter,'
Hammarskjold once said; 'I am not neutral as regards facts.'
A man has to have ideas and ideals. 'But what I do claim is
that even a man who is in that sense not neutral can very well
undertake and carry through neutral actions, because that is
an act of integrity.'[25] U Thant has taken much the same
view, and has equated 'impartiality' with the capacity to undertake neutral actions. Impartiality, in this sense, is the quality
one looks for in a judge.

Two further comments may be made here. First,
international loyalty is 'not the denationalized loyalty of the
man without a country'.[26] There is no room in an international secretariat for Ko-Ko's 'idiot who praises . . . every
country but his own'. To have a sense of loyal attachment to
the culture, traditions, sentiments, and aspirations of one's own

country and people is not incompatible with a proper loyalty to the United Nations.

Secondly, international loyalty includes loyalty to the head of the Secretariat. 'Staff members are subject to the authority of the Secretary-General and . . . are responsible to him in the exercise of their functions.'[27]

All men are not naturally endowed with the qualities that together constitute international loyalty. Impartiality, in particular, is in part a matter of training, discipline, and association with other people. It is for this reason that emphasis has properly been placed on the concept of a career service in the United Nations.*

Some posts must perforce by filled by short-term appointments. Governments and the Secretariat may gain from the fact that national officials may in this way acquire first-hand experience of the work of an international organization. Short-service officials may bring to the Secretariat new ideas and experience acquired in national affairs; they may play a particularly important role at the higher levels of the Secretariat. But against these undoubted advantages must be set three drawbacks.

First, it takes time for even the most highly qualified officials to adapt to the peculiar requirements of an international secretariat. They have to learn new administrative procedures; they have to settle down, perhaps with their families, in a foreign country; they sometimes encounter problems of language, climate, diet, or social custom. A few short-service officials have found these adjustments so trying in the initial stages that they never succeeded in making a full contribution to the work of the Secretariat.

Secondly, some international officials seconded from and expecting to return to national civil services find it more

---

* Staff appointed for periods of less than five years are known as 'fixed-term' staff; I have also used the expressions 'temporary', 'short-service', and 'non-career' staff. For those holding permanent appointments, I have used the term 'career staff'.

difficult to give wholehearted loyalty to an international organization than those having permanent international appointments. Most governments, it is true, regard it as proper that their citizens on secondment to the United Nations should act exclusively in the interests of the Organization. But not all governments, and not all seconded officials, find it easy in all circumstances to take so disinterested an attitude.

A third drawback of secondment is that the qualities of international loyalty come, to a considerable extent, from continuing contact with other people. The personal example of senior officials can have a substantial influence, but equally important are the daily confrontations of different ideas and traditions; the tolerance, respect, and enrichment that come from constant association with people of differing attitudes and cultures; the effect of implementing decisions which almost always contain elements of compromise; the recognition on pragmatic grounds that the United Nations cannot succeed unless officials try to act with fairness.

The proportion of non-career staff has steadily increased from about 11 per cent in 1956 to 29.7 per cent on 31 August 1963, but the proportion varies from region to region. The countries of the communist bloc have urged that the practice of granting career appointments should be terminated forthwith.[28] The Soviet delegation has proposed that only 25 per cent of the staff should be permanent and 75 per cent on short-service contracts.[29]

TABLE I

Non-career staff as percentage of regional totals, 31 August 1963[30]

Western Europe	16·3
Eastern Europe	81·7
Middle East	33·3
Asia and the Far East	29·5
Africa	50·5
Latin America	29·9
North America and the Caribbean	10·7

Various views have been expressed as to a reasonable proportion of non-career staff. The Salary Review Committee recommended in 1956 that the proportion should be 'brought up to say 20 per cent as opportunity offered',[31] and this was approved by the General Assembly in 1957.[32] The Committee of Experts on the Activities and Organization of the Secretariat suggested in 1961 that the proportion might be further increased to 'as much as 25 per cent by the end of 1962',[33] and the figure of 25 per cent was incorporated in a draft resolution submitted by thirteen countries of Africa and Asia during the sixteenth session of the General Assembly.[34] In 1963 the Secretary-General reported that although the proportion of fixed-term staff was then almost 30 per cent, he expected to keep the proportion at about 25 per cent of the total. One way of achieving this would be by the conversion of short-term appointments to career appointments.[35]

It may be doubted whether the proportion of short-term staff should be allowed to rise further. Moreover, there would be much to be said for aiming at appointments of four to five years. Two-year appointments, except for a few special *ad hoc* assignments, are not long enough in most cases to enable an official to make the best contribution to the work of the Secretariat.

I have tried to show that the statesmen who gathered in San Francisco in 1945 were right in formulating so clearly in the Charter the principles on which the Secretariat should function. It has been said there is no compromise, no middle position, between impartiality and partiality, between independence and dependence. If the United Nations is to abandon the principles of Articles 100 and 101 of the Charter, better to abandon them openly than to maintain them in theory while they are being insidiously corroded in practice.

No one can doubt that in fulfilling their tasks, members of the Secretariat have opportunities for showing bias; no one can doubt that mistakes have occurred in the past and will occur in the future. The staff, after all, are human and therefore fallible. It is only prudent to seek safeguards against error, but failure should be regarded as a reason for fresh endeavour rather than for giving up ideals.

A State may use the United Nations to promote its interests through diplomatic representatives who speak and vote in the policy-making organs, who consult the Secretariat, and who engage in quiet diplomacy in the lounges and lobbies. But the Organization cannot achieve its varied purposes unless the decisions of policy-making organs are impartially prepared and implemented. Legitimate national interests cannot be protected by transforming the Secretariat into a congress of ambassadors.

3

THE SECRETARY-GENERAL

IT was always intended that the Secretary-General should be more than an administrator.* This was explicit in the Charter. Indeed, one may classify the responsibilities of the Secretary-General according to constitutional origin as follows:

(*a*) responsibilities arising from his position as chief administrative officer of the Organization and Secretary-General of the General Assembly and the three Councils;

(*b*) such responsibilities as are entrusted to him by the above organs;

(*c*) responsibilities arising from Article 99 of the Charter.

The responsibilities in the first group include those administrative and related duties specified in the Charter and the rules of procedure of the principal and subsidiary organs. When a function is entrusted to the Secretary-General, as the

* Confusion sometimes arises because the words *administrative* and *executive* are used differently in the United Kingdom and the United States. The top echelon of the Civil Service in Britain is called the Administrative Class and the second echelon is called the Executive Class. To an Englishman administrative duties are more onerous and carry more responsibility than executive duties. In the United States, the meanings are reversed; the President exercises executive power. The Preparatory Commission of the United Nations used both words, though without defining them.

responsibility to appoint staff under regulations established by the General Assembly, the legal authority to exercise it belongs exclusively to him.

Responsibilities conferred upon the Secretary-General by United Nations organs under Article 98, whether in general terms by the rules of procedure or by decisions in particular cases, need not be solely administrative in character. During the past decade, the policy-making organs have increasingly entrusted the Secretary-General with diplomatic and operational functions.

It was assumed at San Francisco in 1945 that the chief source of the political power of the Secretary-General lay in Article 99. The Preparatory Commission considered that Article 99 gives to the Secretary-General 'a quite special right which goes beyond any power previously accorded to the head of an international organization';[36] Trygve Lie held that Article 99 'confers upon the Secretary-General . . . world political responsibilities which no individual, no representative of a single nation, ever had before'.[37]

The Evolution of the Office

Lie was never simply an administrator. He concerned himself with political questions and took up definite positions when he considered that the principles of the Charter were at stake, even if this seemed likely to bring him into conflict with one or other of the great powers. His circulation of a memorandum on some legal aspects of the problem of Chinese representation annoyed the United States, and his attitude to the Korean war led to the Soviet decision not to 'recognize' him as Secretary-General. His Twenty-Year Program for achieving peace through the United Nations was an important initiative; it deserved a better reception.

Lie's political and diplomatic activities were broadly in line with ideas that were current when the United Nations was founded. A group of former officials of the League of

Nations had commented in 1944 that little progress in international business was likely unless international officials under-
took negotiating functions,[38] and the Preparatory Commission
foresaw that the Secretary-General would be called upon from
time to time to take decisions which might justly be called
political.[39]   At the same time, direct resort to Article 99 of
the Charter has not played an important part in the evolution
of the Office of Secretary-General.   Lie's intervention in the
Security Council after the Korean War had broken out rein-
forced an initiative which had already been taken, and it was
only later that he claimed that his action on that occasion had
been taken under Article 99.[40]   At the time of the Suez inva-
sion in 1956, Hammarskjold told the Security Council that he
would have used his right to call for an immediate meeting
of the Council had not the United States Government already
taken the initiative.[41]   In the case of the Laotian appeal to the
Secretary-General for a United Nations emergency force to
halt aggression in 1959, Hammarskjold requested the President
of the Security Council to convene the Council to consider
his report on the Laotian appeal, but he made it clear that
this request was not 'based on the explicit rights granted to
the Secretary-General under Article 99 . . .'   To have invoked
Article 99, he said, would necessarily have involved a judgment
as to the facts for which, in the prevailing situation, he did
not have a sufficient basis.[42]   In the Congo case, on the other
hand, Hammarskjold was satisfied that there was a threat, or
a potential threat, to international peace and security,[43] and
he accordingly acted under Article 99.

Article 99 has important implications.   It has been argued
that in order to discharge the responsibilities conferred on him
by this Article, the Secretary-General must have information
which enables him to judge when world peace is threatened.

Dès lors, il a le devoir d'observer l'évolution de la con-
joncture internationale, afin de déceler les dangers qu'elle

peut recéler et les mesurer. Ce qui implique qu'il en ait aussi les moyens. Ceux-ci n'ayant pas été expressément définis par la Charte, ils semblent se réduire à ce qui ne nécessite pas une habilitation juridique particulière: essentiellement, mise à part l'utilisation des informations publiques, les communications qui lui seront faites par les gouvernements ainsi que les contacts qu'il pourra prendre ou accepter, personnellement ou par ses représentants, avec les personnalités les plus diverses, officielles, officieuses ou simples particuliers. Tout au plus peut-on affirmer que l'article 99 exclut toutes restrictions au cercle de ses entretiens et de ses investigations, sauf celles que pourraient lui imposer éventuellement les règles de la 'courtoisie internationale'.[44]

Hammarskjold invoked this idea at the time of the difficulties between Tunisia and France in 1961. He told the Security Council that he had been invited to visit Tunisia by President Bourguiba, but he went on to refer to the implications of Article 99.

... It is obvious that the duties following from this Article cannot be fulfilled unless the Secretary-General, in case of need, is in a position to form a personal opinion about the relevant facts of the situation which may represent such a threat [to international peace and security].[45]

Article 98 of the Charter has, however, provided a constitutional basis for important developments regarding the Office of Secretary-General. It was presumably intended at San Francisco that Article 98 would be used when a policy-making organ wished to entrust the Secretary-General or the Secretariat with a routine administrative function, such as the preparation of a technical report or the collation of the comments of governments. I doubt whether anyone foresaw in 1945 that the Security Council or the General Assembly would one day deal with a grave international crisis by approving a resolution asking the Secretary-General to make such 'arrangements as would adequately help in upholding the purposes and principles of the Charter'.   Yet time and again the policy-making organs have entrusted the Secretary-General with important diplomatic or operational tasks, and in other cases have handed awkward problems to the Secretary-General simply by concluding the consideration of a matter with an understanding that the Secretary-General, in the normal course of his duties, would give the matter attention.[46]

But perhaps the most important development in the role of the Secretary-General has related to functions exercised without the express authority of a policy-making body.   Hammarskjold always distinguished between those specific responsibilities conferred on him by policy-making organs and those general responsibilities which, explicitly or implicitly, attached to the Office of Secretary-General.   When he visited Peking in 1955, following a General Assembly resolution that requested him to seek the release of captured personnel, he was able, in his capacity as Secretary-General of the United Nations and apart from functions entrusted to him by the Assembly, to exchange views with Chinese officials.   When in 1956 he was asked by the Security Council to survey various aspects of compliance with the general armistice agreements in the Middle East, he insisted not only that this request did not detract from his authority under the Charter, but also that it did not add to it.   On the occasion of his reappointment in 1957, he stated that the Secretary-General should act not only when guidance could be found in the Charter or in the decisions of the main organs, but also without such guidance 'should this appear to him necessary in order to help in filling any vacuum that may appear in the systems which the Charter and traditional diplomacy provide for the safeguarding of peace and security'.[47]

Within a year of his reappointment, his interpretation was put to the test.   Lebanon had complained to the Security

Council of intervention in its internal affairs by the United Arab Republic. The Council, acting on a proposal by Sweden, decided to send an observation group to the area in order to ensure that there was no illegal infiltration across the Lebanese borders. A month later, the Lebanese government requested the United States to send forces to help preserve the country's integrity and independence, and the United States complied with the request.

The resulting situation was thereupon considered by the Security Council. A Soviet proposal calling for the immediate withdrawal of United States troops from Lebanon (as well as British troops from Jordan) was defeated, as was a Swedish proposal to suspend the activities of the United Nations Observation Group. The United States proposed that the Secretary-General should make additional arrangements to ensure the independence and integrity of Lebanon, but this was blocked by a Soviet veto.

In this confused and grave situation, Japan submitted what was intended to be a compromise proposal, expressed in the most general terms. This asked the Secretary-General to make arrangements forthwith for such measures as he might consider necessary with a view to ensuring the integrity and independence of Lebanon, thus making possible the withdrawal of United States forces from that country. This received ten affirmative votes, but the negative Soviet vote constituted a veto.

Here was a vacuum *par excellence*, and Hammarskjold had no hesitation in acting. His statement to the Security Council conveys most vividly his sense of responsibility.

The Security Council has just failed to take additional action in the grave emergency facing us. However, the responsibility of the United Nations to make all efforts to live up to the purposes and principles of the Charter remains. . . .

In a statement before this Council on 31 October 1956, I said that the discretion and impartiality imposed on the Secretary-General by the character of his immediate task must not degenerate into a policy of expediency. On a later occasion—it was 26 September 1957—I said in a statement before the General Assembly that I believed it to be the duty of the Secretary-General 'to use his office and, indeed, the machinery of the Organization to its utmost capacity and to the full extent permitted at each stage by practical circumstances.' I added that I believed that it is in keeping with the philosophy of the Charter that the Secretary-General also should be expected to act without any guidance from the Assembly or the Security Council should this appear to him necessary towards helping to fill any vacuum that may appear in the systems which the Charter and traditional diplomacy provide for the safeguarding of peace and security. . . .

I am sure that I will be acting in accordance with the wishes of the members of the Council if I, therefore, use all opportunities offered to the Secretary-General, within the limits set by the Charter and towards developing the United Nations effort, so as to help to prevent a further deterioration of the situation in the Middle East. . . .

First of all . . . this will mean the further development of the Observation Group [in Lebanon]. The Council will excuse me for not being able to spell out at this moment what it may mean beyond that. . . .[48]

Limits of Parliamentary Diplomacy

The fact is that policy-making organs do not always respond to a crisis smoothly or swiftly; parliamentary diplomacy has its limitations. When tension arose between Cambodia and Thailand in 1958, the two governments agreed that the dispute should not go to a policy-making organ in the first instance. They asked the Secretary-General to designate a representative to help them in finding a solution. This was done without the formal approval of the Security Council, though with the knowledge of its members.* 'Such actions by the Secretary-General', reported Hammarskjold, 'fall within the competence of his Office and are . . . in other respects also in strict accordance with the Charter, when they serve its purpose'. The method he had used, he said, avoided public debate in a policy-making organ which might have increased the difficulties. Member States might well have been hesitant to give explicit prior approval to an action without fuller knowledge of the facts. The evolution of the Office of Secretary-General represented 'an intensification and a broadening of the interplay' between the policy-making organs and the Secretariat, while maintaining the principle that the activities of the United Nations are 'wholly dependent on decisions of the Governments'.[49]

In 1959, Hammarskjold again took action on his own responsibility in a difficult situation, even though the matter had come before the Security Council. The Laotian government requested that a United Nations force be sent to Laos to halt aggression. The Security Council met at Hammarskjold's request and decided to appoint a sub-committee to inquire into the situation.† The sub-committee reported on 5 November 1959, and three days later Hammarskjold announced that, 'taking into account his duties under the Charter, and all the information at present available', he had decided to pay a personal visit to Laos.[50] Later, within the framework

---

* In 1962, Cambodia and Thailand asked U Thant to appoint a personal representative to assist them regarding further differences which had arisen; U Thant complied with the request.

† The Soviet Union regarded this as a substantive rather than a procedural question, and therefore as subject to the veto. The Council decided by 10 votes to 1 (the Soviet Union) that the decision was only procedural, but the Soviet Union argued that this preliminary question should also be subject to the veto, in accordance with the four-power statement at San Francisco of 7 June 1945. The President of the Council ruled, however, that the resolution had been validly adopted.

of the United Nations technical assistance program, he appointed a special consultant for the co-ordination of United Nations activities in Laos. The Soviet government took the position that Hammarskjold's visit and his subsequent actions were 'designed to cover by the name of the United Nations further interference of the Western powers in Laos. . . .'[51]

U Thant has continued the policy of taking diplomatic and political initiatives. In 1962, on his own responsibility, he acceded to a request from the Netherlands and Indonesia that the United Nations should establish a temporary executive authority for West New Guinea (West Irian).[52] The following year he agreed to the despatch of United Nations observers to the Yemen, and the matter was discussed and approved by the Security Council only as a result of a request from the Soviet government.[53] Also in 1963, at the request of Malaya, Indonesia, and the Philippines, he agreed to 'ascertain the wishes' of the people of Sabah (North Borneo) and Sarawak regarding the future status of the two territories.[54]

There have been, then, two parallel and related trends. First, policy-making organs have increasingly entrusted the Secretary-General with broad diplomatic and operational functions; secondly, the Secretaries-General have used to the full the resources of the Office in the exercise of independent initiatives designed to further the purposes and principles of the Charter. And it cannot be denied that the totality of these developments has given to the Office of Secretary-General a character that had not been foreseen by the founders of the Organization. Indeed, Hammarskjold had gone so far as to describe the office as 'a one-man "executive", with explicit authority in the administrative field, supplementary to, but not overlapping the authority of either the [Security] Council or the Assembly'.[55] In his speech at Oxford in 1961, he stated that the conception of the office of Secretary-General originated in the United States.

The United States gave serious consideration to the idea that the Organization should have a President as well as a Secretary-General. Subsequently, it was decided to propose only a single officer, but one in whom there would be combined both the political and executive functions of a President with the internal administrative functions that were previously accorded to a Secretary-General.[56]

The Secretary-General is, of course, appointed by the will of Member States, and his independence is guaranteed by the Charter stipulation that he shall neither seek nor receive instructions from any source external to the United Nations. If Member States had wished to prevent the strengthening of the office of Secretary-General, they could have done so. They were, however, glad to leave things to the Secretary-General when parliamentary diplomacy was not enough.

The trouble was that parliamentary diplomacy had been becoming more and more parliamentary, and less and less diplomatic. Delegates were sometimes in danger of forgetting the purposes of the United Nations, so admirably set forth in the first Article of the Charter; attention, instead, was increasingly directed, not to purposes, but to methods. Debate was coming to be thought of as an end in itself; a vote was mistaken for action.

The chief purpose of parliamentary diplomacy (though not always the only one) is to cause a reassessment of national interests in the light of the national interests of others. The various elements that together constitute parliamentary diplomacy are occasionally sufficient in themselves to bring the actions of nations into harmony. This seems to have been the case, for example, in the General Assembly's consideration of the Syrian-Turkish tension in 1957 and in the Security Council's consideration of the Sudan-Egyptian border dispute in 1958. But sometimes more is needed. In a variety of circumstances, it has been found useful to go further, and to inject the physical presence of the United Nations into situations of difficulty or tension. Such a United Nations presence symbolizes the concern of the international community, but it may do more than that. A government may refuse to comply with a decision of a policy-making organ but would think twice before taking action which would bring it into direct, on-the-spot conflict with representatives of the international community. A United Nations presence creates conditions in which it is difficult to assault the principles of the United Nations without at the same time assaulting its representatives.

The 'presence' of the United Nations may consist of the Secretary-General, or one or more representatives appointed by him, or by a policy-making organ; it may consist of an inter-governmental committee; it may consist of persons or contingents, loaned by governments, for observation or police duties; it may consist of a section of the Secretariat with special regional or functional responsibilities. The form of the presence has to be tailored to the needs of each situation.

In practice there are, naturally, limits to what a United Nations 'presence' can do under Chapter VI of the Charter. It cannot enter territory without the consent of the government concerned. It must have the freedom of movement and the facilities necessary to undertake the tasks committed to it. It must to some extent operate independently of the host government, and yet without becoming a rival authority. It must abstain from actions taken to influence the internal political situation.

The United Nations operations initiated in the Middle East following the crises of 1956 and 1958 created important precedents. In both cases, considerable discretion was given to the Secretary-General in implementing the decisions of policy-making organs. The 'presences' were established in accordance with his proposals, and he was made the agent of the Organization in attempting to secure certain objectives.

43

The Congo

The Congo case has been the most intricate and intractable in which the United Nations has been involved. The lack of preparation for independence and the unexpected speed of the transfer of sovereignty resulted in a vacuum that Congolese nationalists were not in a position to fill. The question in July 1960 was whether the United Nations could stabilize and insulate the situation for an interim period until adequate and united Congolese leadership had emerged. The Congo operation has been criticized from almost every conceivable point of view, but the critics should bear in mind that the operation had to be conducted in conformity with principles that had been accepted as valid in earlier and very different operations, and that actions taken in the Congo would become precedents for the future. It is easier to complain that this or that political result was not achieved than to lay down an acceptable code for United Nations action, particularly in relation to the internal affairs of a State.

Moreover, the decisions of the Security Council and the General Assembly regarding the Congo did not always give clear guidance to those on the spot. How was the Secretary-General to interpret the mandate to assist the Government of the Congo if more than one authority claimed to be that government? How was it possible for the United Nations both to safeguard the unity of the Congo in the face of secessionist activities and at the same time to abstain from any action that would influence any internal conflict? Did the United Nations mandate to prevent civil war extend to resisting by force Central Government troops which might try to enter secessionist areas if their declared purpose was to restore the territorial integrity and unity of the Congo? At what point did the use of force, as a last resort, become necessary? Nor should it be forgotten that many Member States were content to give instructions to the Secretary-General (and, indeed, to complain at the way he carried them out) while denying him the material resources and diplomatic backing he was entitled to expect.

It was the course of events in the Congo that sparked off the Soviet onslaught on Hammarskjold. Until 1959, the Soviet Union appeared to trust and respect him. In spite of Hammarskjold's support for the idea of a committee to investigate the situation following the Hungarian revolt in 1956, Khrushchev proposed in 1958 that the Secretary-General should participate in a meeting of heads of government on the Middle East. Although there was some Soviet criticism of Hammarskjold's activities in connection with the Laotian appeal for a United Nations force, the attack was relatively muted, and after Hammarskjold had invoked Article 99 of the Charter in connection with the Congo in July 1960, the Soviet Union supported the first three resolutions asking the Secretary-General to implement the Security Council's decisions. Within a few weeks, however, the Soviet government had launched a bitter personal attack on Hammarskjold. Khrushchev complained, first, that Hammarskjold had disregarded decisions of United Nations organs; second, and more generally, that he had supported the colonialist and capitalist States in the Congo and was biased against the Soviet Union and its allies. Khrushchev said bluntly that the countries of the Soviet bloc no longer trusted Hammarskjold and called on him to resign. Later, the Soviet government went even further and demanded that Hammarskjold be dismissed from his post.[57]

But the Soviet government wanted more than simply the removal of Hammarskjold. Khrushchev maintained that there were basic faults in the structure of the United Nations. The concrete reality of the present world, he said, is that it comprises three groups of States: the communist States; the neutralist, unaligned, or uncommitted States; and States which he described as belonging to Western military blocs. The post of Secretary-General should be abolished, he said; 'the executive organ of the United Nations should reflect the real situation that obtains in the world today'. In place of a single Secretary-General there should be a collective executive organ consisting of 'persons representing the States belonging to the three basic groups'. The crux of the matter, said Khrushchev, is not what should be the name of the new executive body but that this executive organ should 'represent' the States belonging to the three groups, thus guaranteeing that the executive work of the United Nations 'would not be carried out to the detriment of any one of these groups of States'.[58]

What had happened between 9 August 1960, when the Soviet delegation voted for the resolution confirming the authority already given to the Secretary-General in the Congo and entrusting additional responsibilities to him, and 23 September, when Khrushchev attacked Hammarskjold from the rostrum of the General Assembly? Was the 'troika' proposal a hasty and petulant response to particular United Nations actions in the Congo which had displeased the Soviet government, or did it represent a premeditated demand based on a long-term Soviet interpretation of general trends in world affairs?

It is not in dispute that the Soviet government suffered a setback in the Congo, but it is significant that the 'troika' idea was linked closely to possible future developments in relation to disarmament and the peace-keeping functions of the United Nations. The particular form the proposal took was probably based on the following considerations. First, in the light of the growth of the Secretary-General's independent exercise of those functions which the Soviet Union regarded as the sole responsibility of the Security Council, the Soviet government wished to have means to prevent action by the Secretariat which it regarded as inimical to its interests. Secondly, the Soviet government had for some years claimed that the Soviet bloc should have a position of parity with the Western group in United Nations organs. Finally, the Soviet government considered that the concept of impartiality was merely a mask to conceal the fact that the Secretariat promoted Western policies.[59]

This is not the occasion to attempt to write an account of the United Nations operation in the Congo[60] or of Hammarskjold's service as Secretary-General of the United Nations, but I am convinced that no man could have acted with greater independence, integrity, and impartiality than Hammarskjold, that no man could have shown a higher sense of international responsibility.

The United Nations responded to the request from the government of the Congo on the basis of complete impartiality and neutrality regarding internal political differences. The United Nations Emergency Force in the Middle East had been based on the same principle that it would never be used to enforce any particular political solution or to influence the political balance in any way.[61] The United Nations Observation Group in Lebanon similarly sought to avoid any partisan act, even during conditions of civil war. The Security Council's resolution of 9 August 1960 regarding the Congo reaffirmed that 'the United Nations Force in the Congo will not be a party to or in any way intervene or be used to influence the outcome of any internal conflict, constitutional or otherwise'.[62]

It was not possible, at the time the Congo operation was launched by the Security Council, to foresee how difficult it would become to interpret the original mandate. The United Nations was sending a force to the Congo, not to secure and supervise the cessation of hostilities as had been the task of UNEF in the Middle East, nor to prevent infiltration across borders as had been the case with the Observation Group in Lebanon. The Security Council decided in its first resolution to furnish military assistance to the government of the Congo, and called for the withdrawal of Belgian forces. The United Nations Force was to provide the government of an independent State with military aid. The principle that the United

Nations Force would not influence internal conflicts in the Congo became increasingly difficult to interpret and implement, particularly when secessionist and other groups in the Congo received encouragement and support from outside.

The crisis leading to the events of which the Soviet Union complained broke on 5 September. The Congo was on the verge of economic and political collapse. The Prime Minister, Patrice Lumumba, had clashed with Hammarskjold about the way the United Nations had handled the Katanga problem, and had then openly taken military help from the Soviet Union and other non-UN sources. This brought to a head differences within the Congolese government, and on the evening of 5 September, President Kasavubu declared over the radio that he had dismissed the government of Lumumba and had invited Joseph Iléo to form a new government. Lumumba thereupon called a meeting of the Council of Ministers, which decided to depose Kasavubu.

Léopoldville was in an explosive and tense condition, with two rival groups trying to mobilize support among the population. The attempt to insulate the Congo from disruptive external forces was being impeded by the fact that Belgium was openly supporting one faction in the Congo and the Soviet Union another. On the day of Lumumba's dismissal, Hammarskjold had addressed a blunt communication to the Belgian Delegation in New York on the delay in the evacuation of Belgian troops from the Congo and an equally blunt communication to the Soviet Delegation about the arrival in the Congo of Soviet Ilyushin planes, in defiance of the Security Council's resolutions.[63]

United Nations representatives in the Congo had been instructed to avoid any action by which, directly or indirectly, openly or by implication, they might pass judgment on any internal conflict, and they found themselves in a situation in which inaction as well as action was likely to be interpreted by one side or the other as contravening this principle. In an effort to prevent an outbreak of violence in Léopoldville, the United Nations Special Representative temporarily closed the radio station and the airport. It was his intention that the action would be impartial in its consequences; Kasavubu and Lumumba were to be equally affected by it, although in the event the action worked against Lumumba. These emergency measures were taken without consulting Hammarskjold, who was at Headquarters in New York.

Hammarskjold clearly faced a painful dilemma. While he could hardly disavow a decision taken in good faith by a trusted colleague at a time of acute difficulty, to endorse the action would risk bringing him into open conflict with influential Member States. Hammarskjold did not hesitate to take that risk and stated plainly that he fully endorsed the action.

After his dismissal, Lumumba sought and was granted United Nations protection in Léopoldville. At the end of November, Lumumba left the residence in which he had been guarded by the United Nations, and some days later he was arrested by the Congolese National Army. In the middle of January 1961, Lumumba was transferred to Elisabethville; on 10 February it was announced by the authorities in Katanga that Lumumba had 'escaped', and shortly afterward it became known that he had been killed.

After Lumumba's arrest, United Nations representatives in the Congo had tried to secure all possible legal and humanitarian protection for him. When he was transferred to Elisabethville, the Secretary-General and his representative in the Congo exercised all the influence possible for his return to Léopoldville and for the application of normal legal rules in the protection of his interests. No attempt was made by the United Nations to obtain his release by forcible means, since such action was considered to have been beyond the mandate conferred by the Security Council at that time.

The murder of Lumumba was—to use Hammarskjold's words—a revolting crime; it was also a political tragedy. But when Khrushchev first attacked Hammarskjold, Lumumba was still alive, enjoying the protection of United Nations forces. The launching of the 'troika' proposal preceded the assassination of Lumumba by about four months.

The Security Council met in September 1960, but by now the unanimity of the great powers could no longer be obtained. Following the veto of a resolution sponsored by Tunisia and Ceylon, an emergency special session of the General Assembly was called under the Uniting for Peace procedure. The countries of the Soviet bloc attacked Hammarskjold's handling of the Congo operation, but the Assembly voted by 70 votes to none (the Soviet bloc, France, and South Africa abstaining) to confirm and strengthen the Secretary-General's mandate. The break with Hammarskjold was to come three days later.

The Troika

Khrushchev attacked Hammarskjold for his conduct of the Congo operation, but it is significant that whenever he addressed the General Assembly on the subject of tripartite administration in 1960, he immediately proceeded to discuss disarmament and the use of international forces for maintaining peace.

The United Nations Secretariat must therefore be adapted even now to the conditions which will come into being as disarmament decisions are implemented. An identical point of view has emerged . . . regarding the necessity of following up an agreement on disarmament with the establishment of armed forces of all countries, under international control, to be used by the United Nations in accordance with the decision of the Security Council.[64]

It has been said that, after an agreement on disarmament has been reached, international armed forces should be formed. We are, in principle, in agreement with this.

But the question arises, who will command these forces?
The United Nations Secretary-General? . . . Is it really
permissible for the fate of millions to be dependent on
the actions of the one man occupying that post? . . . There
can be no disarmament, there can be no international
armed forces, in the absence of guarantees for all three
groups [of States] against the misuse of these armed
forces.[65]

To demand guarantees against misuse is legitimate;
the Soviet government is not alone in making this demand.
But the proposal for a collective executive body, in the form
in which it was presented, went much further. Each member
of the proposed triumvirate would be able, in certain circumstances, to prevent the decisions of policy-making organs from
being implemented, either by outright veto or by the use of
delaying tactics. What other interpretation can there be of
the following extract from Khrushchev's first statement on
the subject?

We consider it advisable to set up, in the place of a Secretary-General who is at present the interpreter and executor
of the decisions of the General Assembly and the Security
Council, a collective executive organ of the United Nations
consisting of three persons each of whom would represent
a certain group of States. That would provide a definite
guarantee that the work of the United Nations executive
organ would not be carried on to the detriment of any
one of these groups of States. The United Nations executive organ would then be a genuinely democratic organ;
it would really guard the interests of all States Members
of the United Nations. . . .[66]

It is true that the Soviet government never formally
stated that each member of a three-man executive would in
all circumstances have the right of veto, but it is a reasonable
assumption and will no doubt be generally accepted until it

is expressly denied. Indeed, in an official elaboration of its views, the Soviet government did not challenge an allegation by the United States that the 'troika' proposal would be tantamount to the introduction of the right of veto into the administrative realm.[67]

The veto, even if it is called the rule of unanimity, is essentially negative. Its effect is not to foster cooperation; it is to prevent action. Indeed, if the problem were simply to prevent the United Nations from acting to the detriment of any State or group of States, the solution would be to extend the veto to all Members in all organs of the United Nations. The heart of the matter is whether we will advance toward the goal of a secure international order by limiting or by extending the right of States to act arbitrarily in pursuit of objectives they regard as legitimate.

The veto in the Security Council can prevent the initiation of action, but it cannot ensure its termination. Although a policy-making organ of the United Nations can withdraw a mandate as easily as it can confer it, once a decision has been taken, it is valid until rescinded. An operation authorized by the Security Council cannot be stopped by a veto if one of the permanent members later finds the course of events not to its liking. The return of the Soviet representative to the Security Council after the boycott in 1950 could not lead to the cancellation of the earlier decisions to resist aggression in Korea. In the Lebanon operation of 1958, the veto of a proposal that the Secretary-General should make arrangements for such measures as he might consider necessary to ensure the integrity and independence of the Lebanon did not annul the original decision to send an observation group to ensure that there was no illegal infiltration across the Lebanese borders. When the Soviet Union became displeased with events in the Congo, it was unable to use its veto to terminate the United Nations operation.

The situation in the General Assembly is similar. An

operation may be launched by a two-thirds majority of those Member States present and voting; one-third of the Members plus one can prevent a decision. But an operation, once under way, can be halted only by an express decision by a two-thirds majority.

Interpreting the Mandate

Difficulties undoubtedly arise when resolutions entrusting the Secretary-General with broad responsibilities are expressed in vague general terms. It is, of course, impossible to foresee all eventualities; some matters must be left for later interpretation or decision. But there is all the difference in the world between a prudent avoidance of precision when all the circumstances cannot be foreseen and the transfer of total responsibility for decision and action to the Secretary-General because a policy-making organ has failed to agree on what should be done.

Agreement depends on negotiation, and negotiation takes time. The General Assembly, in particular, now tries to do more than it can do well. Time can be saved for the more important matters only by the exercise of greater discrimination regarding the agenda and a decrease of what in the British House of Commons is called 'irrelevance or tedious repetition'.

Public debate is an essential part of parliamentary diplomacy, but its limitations must be recognized. After the parties to a dispute have made initial statements in a public session of a policy-making organ, efforts to narrow the differences can be undertaken in private. The use of special rapporteurs, both to elucidate the issues and to make proposals for a solution, was one of the more successful practices of the League of Nations, and it is a pity that United Nations organs have not adopted the practice. Individuals can nearly always perform this function more effectively than committees.[68] This is not to say that there is some magic formula for ensuring the sort of agreement that can be embodied in an unambiguous resolution, but there are some methods that tend toward this result and some that do not.

Even when resolutions are fairly precise, later developments may pose problems for the Secretariat which were not foreseen when the resolution was adopted. In some cases, the Secretary-General may be able to consult an advisory committee of Member States; in other cases, he may refer the matter to the policy-making organ for clarification or extension of the original mandate. When differences arose between Hammarskjold and Lumumba in August 1960, Hammarskjold called for a meeting of the Security Council to clarify its attitude.[69] At a later stage in the Congo operation, Hammarskjold made it clear that fresh decisions by the Council were needed. 'It cannot shirk its responsibilities by expecting from the Secretariat action on which it is not prepared to take decisions itself.'[70] The Council, after debate, adopted a resolution authorizing the use of force, if necessary, in the last resort, in order to prevent civil war in the Congo.

The Secretary-General, however, may occasionally be confronted with issues regarding which it will be impossible to secure a clear judgment from an advisory committee or a policy-making organ. In such circumstances, Hammarskjold was prepared to act 'on his own risk, but with as faithful an interpretation of the instructions, rights and obligations of the Organization as possible in view of international law and the decisions already taken'.[71] It is no criticism of Hammarskjold to suggest that no Secretary-General should, in present circumstances, be expected to decide such questions 'on his own risk'.

The fact that it is difficult to delineate the scope within which a Secretary-General may properly exercise initiative should not be a reason for replacing a single, independent, and impartial officer by a triumvirate of ideological representatives. Although there was a widespread sentiment in 1960 that some organizational changes in the Secretariat were desirable, the Soviet proposal for a tripartite executive evoked virtually no support outside the Soviet bloc. What amounted to a vote of confidence in Hammarskjold took place at the fourth emergency special session of the Assembly in September 1960, and this was confirmed the following April. It had been proposed to omit the words 'by the Secretary-General' from a draft resolution asking that 'necessary and effective measures be taken' to prevent the introduction of arms and supplies to the Congo. A roll-call vote was requested by Guinea, and the proposal not to refer to the Secretary-General was rejected by 83 votes to 11, with 5 abstentions. The minority comprised the nine Soviet bloc States of Eastern Europe, together with Cuba and Guinea. This was a striking expression of confidence in Hammarskjold.

When Hammarskjold died, the Soviet Union could have proposed that a three-man executive organ be created, and it could have threatened to veto in the Security Council any attempt to appoint a single successor. One reason why the Soviet Union was prepared to agree to the appointment of U Thant was presumably the knowledge that the 'troika' idea would have received no more than a dozen or so votes in the General Assembly. Soviet protests about decisions taken in the Secretariat in the interval between the death of Hammarskjold and the appointment of U Thant were relatively perfunctory.[72]

The terms of U Thant's appointment do not derogate from the principles of the Charter. The text of his speech of acceptance may have been known in advance to a number of people, but the speech was naturally not delivered until after he had been appointed. His reference to Article 101 of the Charter and to his intention to designate a limited number of advisers maintained the important principle that it is the Secretary-General who appoints the staff. U Thant emphasized that the arrangement was without prejudice to such future changes as might be necessary.

U Thant has shown himself a worthy successor to Lie and Hammarskjold—courteous, fair-minded, and firm. His task is not easy. In addition to the normally heavy responsibilities of the Office, he must guide and inspire the Secretariat during a difficult process of reorganization, and at a time when the United Nations as a whole faces serious political and financial problems. He must establish an effective system of consultation at the top level of the Secretariat.

Hammarskjold never succeeded in creating a satisfactory system of consultation and collaboration at the senior level of the Secretariat. He handled much of the political work himself, with the help of a few colleagues on the thirty-eighth floor; the Department of Political and Security Council Affairs tended to lack drive and purpose. The meetings of Under-Secretaries, held on Friday mornings, were primarily occasions for reporting information rather than for resolving issues. Hammarskjold dealt with difficulties by direct discussion with the officials concerned.

A similar problem had beset the League of Nations, and the idea of constituting an advisory group for the Secretary-General of the League was frequently mooted. A former League official, after referring to certain 'arbitrary measures taken by the second Secretary-General during the critical months of 1940', comments as follows:

> It is the almost generally accepted opinion of persons with inside experience that, basically, the head of the international administration must retain the sole and final responsibility but that his relationship to his principal collaborators should be formalized by the creation of an advisory body. . . . Such an advisory body would . . . fulfill an important function without hampering the unity of control and moment.[73]

It is clear from the Charter that it is for the Secretary-General to decide a matter of this kind. Every Secretary-General will take account of both legal and political considerations, and will be influenced by his own temperament and by the personalities of his senior colleagues. Some tasks can be delegated; some responsibilities can be shared; but in the last resort, there are duties that have been expressly conferred on the Secretary-General, who is the only official of the Secretariat appointed by Member States.

Relations with Member States

Apart from his varied internal responsibilities of an administrative and related character, the Secretary-General must seek to establish relations of trust with Member States. We take it for granted nowadays that this means, in the first place, relations with permanent missions at Headquarters, but this would have shocked Sir Eric Drummond. Drummond was very much opposed to permanent diplomatic missions attached to the League of Nations, as he considered it essential that the League Secretariat should have direct access to governments and should not have to go through intermediaries. He also feared that the staff of permanent missions would be used to represent governments on League organs on matters for which they were not technically qualified.[74] The first of Drummond's anxieties has not, in the event, proved to be well founded; indeed, the institution of permanent missions has, in important respects, facilitated contacts between the Secretariat and Member States.

Relations between the Secretary-General and the permanent missions are largely of an informal kind, but formal institutions of consultation are also needed. Because the General Assembly is so large, select committees of Member States have proved useful in connection with some of the functions entrusted to the Secretary-General. Advisory committees exist for the operations in the Middle East and the Congo, and there is also an advisory committee on scientific questions. Certain principles regarding the composition and working of these committees may be suggested.

(1) They should be as representative as possible of the States providing the operation in question with the men, materials, logistical support, finance, and diplomatic backing.

(2) In order to facilitate effective working, such committees should be kept small; fifteen should normally be regarded as the maximum size.

(3) They should meet in private; there should normally be no voting; the chairman should sum up the feeling of the meeting, and any member should have the right to place a dissenting opinion on the record or, in the case of acute dissatisfaction, to request a meeting of the appropriate policy-making organ to resolve the issue.

When broad responsibilities are committed to the Secretary-General by the policy-making organs and unforeseen questions of interpretation are possible, it might be useful to have some procedure analogous to that used in a number of national political systems for the scrutiny of delegated legislation. In the United Kingdom, a representative committee of the House of Commons examines each exercise of delegated legislation with a view to determining whether the attention of the House should be drawn to it on any one of a number of grounds. These include:

(1) that it has financial implications;

(2) that it appears to make some unusual or unexpected use of the powers conferred;

(3) that there appears to have been an unjustifiable delay in publishing the relevant documents;

(4) that for any special reason the form or purport calls for elucidation.[75]

Such a scrutinizing procedure does not require that the merits of the original decision should be reviewed, only that the body conferring the mandate should be informed if the authority appears to have been improperly exercised.

The United Nations is an instrument, admittedly im-
perfect, with which Member States seek to mitigate the hazards
of what would otherwise be international anarchy—if by anarchy
is meant the absence of government. No particular form of
machinery will ensure that a consensus will emerge among
the States of which the Organization is composed; but when
a consensus does emerge, when a policy-making organ is able
to make a clear decision, it is essential that it be carried out
by the Secretary-General and staff in a spirit of independence,
impartiality, and integrity. To replace a single, independent
Secretary-General by a political triumvirate, each member
armed with a veto on administrative or executive action, would
render the United Nations helpless in any situation in which
one of the triumvirs considered that, in order to 'represent' a
group of States, he had to block a particular action—and what
situation can be conceived in which this possibility would not
exist? The 'troika' would confine the Organization to being
a forum for conference diplomacy and could bring to a halt
a wide range of operational activities, first in the political field
and later in the economic and social fields also. It would be
the medium and smaller nations whose interests would be
most adversely affected.

4

THE SECRETARIAT: SOME ORGANIZATIONAL QUESTIONS

IN the last chapter I was concerned mainly with the role of the Secretary-General in the political field, but the Secretariat is not a one-man operation, nor is it exclusively concerned with political questions. There are, in fact, nearly 6,000 staff members of the United Nations. Of some 2,000 established posts of professional and higher level, more than half are for interpreters and translators and for general administrative services. Of the remaining professional posts, 85 per cent are for economic and social affairs, 3 per cent for trusteeship and related matters, 4 per cent for legal questions, and only 8 per cent for political work.

The United Nations has been entrusted with a diversity of functions, and this is reflected in the duties of staff members. They service the policy-making bodies by preparing and circulating relevant documents, providing the technical services for meetings, assisting in planning and organization for the proper conduct of proceedings, and following up the implementation of resolutions. They prepare reports and studies, and undertake investigations. They conduct correspondence and maintain liaison with outside bodies. They advise and assist governments concerning matters of economic and social development. They administer the finances and property of the United Nations, procure supplies, maintain records, and provide factual information on the Organization's activities.

TABLE 2

United Nations Secretariat, 1964[76]

	Secretary-General and Under-Secretaries	Directors and Principal Officers	Other Professional Staff	Total Professional and higher level Staff	General Service Staff
Executive Office of Secretary-General	2	4	13	19	24
Legal Office and International Court of Justice	2	6	41	49	38
Political	3	10	49	62	37
Dependent territories	1	2	24	27	17
Economic and Social Affairs	8	61	840	909	1056
Public Information	1	13	157	171	324
Administrative Services	5	39	798	842	1680
Field Service	—	—	—	—	208
Undistributed	—	3	7	10	(10)
Total	22	138	1929	2089	3374

It is only in books that a neat distinction can be made between policy and administration. The primary tasks of the Secretariat are administrative, but there is scope at all levels for the intelligent exercise of initiative which in no way derogates from the powers of the policy-making bodies.

The Secretariat encounters problems that afflict any large bureaucracy; in addition, there are difficulties peculiar to international organizations—the harmonizing of different administrative traditions, the possibility of conflicting loyalties, and the absence of a cohesive political executive comparable to a national cabinet, to name but three.

Some staff members come from countries in which the civil service is conceived as a permanent institution, wholly independent of politics, serving the political leadership of the day loyally and impartially. This conception requires a career service, recruited exclusively on merit, with regular promotion, and with security of tenure except in cases of scandalous misconduct. Other staff members come from countries in which the civil service is a political institution. In such a system, the executive leadership may consist not only of persons appointed from the civil service but also persons brought in from parliamentary, party, or other external posts.

It is rare to find either system fully realized, but they are recognizably different, and persons appointed to the staff of the United Nations will have been influenced to some degree by one or the other tradition. The Secretaries-General, in accordance with the Charter, have tried to develop a Secretariat independent of politics and serving the policy-making organs loyally and impartially, while at the same time appointing to the staff men and women from countries whose governments question or reject the validity of these ideals.

In 1960–61, the question of the organization and activities of the Secretariat was the subject of a special review.[77] The Advisory Committee on Administrative and Budgetary Questions (hereafter referred to as the Advisory Committee), which examines the budget and assists the Assembly's Fifth Committee, suggested that there might be 'some advantage in considering at that time [1961] the desirability of having another over-all review of the organization of the Secretariat'.[78] A hint of this kind would naturally appeal to economy-minded delegations, which would hope that a review committee of the kind suggested would save more money than it would cost. A formal proposal to set up an *ad hoc* committee on the Secretariat was sponsored by the United States, Britain, the Soviet Union, and the United Arab Republic—an unusual manifestation of harmony. The four-power proposal was approved unanimously.[79]

From the beginning, problems were encountered. The

Secretary-General had been asked to appoint a Committee of six persons 'with due regard to geographical distribution' but it soon became evident that six posts were insufficient to provide adequate geographical distribution. The Secretary-General therefore appointed eight persons on a provisional basis.* This action was later confirmed by the Assembly.

Between the time of its appointment and its main meetings in the spring of 1961, the nature of the assignments given to the Committee was affected by the radical proposals of the Soviet Union for reform of the United Nations.† The Committee could hardly ignore the major political issues raised by the 'troika' proposal; all the same, a committee of experts can make a useful contribution to controversial political questions only if it is able to isolate issues susceptible of technical treatment.[80]

The Committee was asked 'to work together with the Secretary-General. . . .'[81] The Secretary-General set up a Secretariat working party to assist the Committee in its work, appointed two special consultants, and assigned staff from the Secretariat to work with the Committee. Personal

---

* The original members of the Committee were: Guillaume Georges-Picot, former Permanent Representative of France to the United Nations and formerly Assistant Secretary-General for the Departments of Economic Affairs and Social Affairs, *Chairman*; Francisco Urrutia, former Permanent Representative of Colombia to the United Nations, *Rapporteur*; A. A. Fomin, Soviet Ministry of Foreign Affairs, former member of U.S.S.R. Permanent Mission to the United Nations and Delegate to the General Assembly; Omar Loutfi, Permanent Representative of the United Arab Republic to the United Nations; Sir Harold Parker, member of International Civil Service Advisory Board, former Permanent Secretary to the United Kingdom Ministry of Defence: Alex Quaison-Sackey, Permanent Representative of Ghana to the United Nations; C. S. Venkatachar, High Commissioner of India to Canada; Herman B. Wells, President of the University of Indiana, former member of the United States Delegation to the General Assembly. On 6 February 1961, A. A. Roshchin, Alternate Soviet Representative to the fifteenth session of the General Assembly, and L. M. Goodrich, Professor of International Organization and Administration, Columbia University, were appointed by the Secretary-General to replace Fomin and Wells, respectively.

† The Committee was given additional tasks during the fifteenth session of the General Assembly (1960). See Appendix F, pp. 112-13.

discussions between Hammarskjold and the Committee were, however, confined to two meetings, and Hammarskjold commented later that part of the Committee's report 'does not reflect in any sense the views that the Secretary-General expressed to the Committee. . . .'[82] Published records do not indicate why the cooperation between Hammarskjold and the Committee, which the General Assembly had envisaged, did not materialize.

During the course of the fifteenth session of the General Assembly, Hammarskjold invited three past Presidents of the General Assembly (Lester B. Pearson of Canada, Prince Wan Waithayakon of Thailand, and Victor Andrés Belaúnde of Peru) to examine certain weaknesses in the organization of the Secretariat at the Under-Secretary level and to suggest ways and means of meeting the problem. The report of the three past Presidents was annexed to the report of the Committee of Experts, but none of the members of the Committee endorsed the recommendations of the past Presidents.[83] These latter recommendations were, however, very much in line with Hammarskjold's own ideas.

The Committee of Experts was divided on most of the major issues with which it was concerned. Separate statements by one or more experts were incorporated in the body of the report, and on the last day of the Committee's meetings, the Soviet expert asked that the report include a separate appendix containing his own views. As a consequence, three other members of the Committee also appended separate statements.

I turn now to three of the matters to which the Committee of Experts gave special attention.

Organization at the Top Level

The Charter does not specify how the top level of the Secretariat shall be organized. China suggested at Dumbarton Oaks that six deputy secretaries-general (four being nationals of the major powers) should be elected by the Security Council with approval of the General Assembly, but the suggestion was not pressed. The Soviet Union raised the matter again at San Francisco, and the other Sponsoring Powers agreed to a modification of the Dumbarton Oaks proposals. The medium and smaller States were, however, opposed to anything that might increase the control exercised by the major powers, and the revised proposal of the Big Four was not adopted.[84] The Charter provides simply that the staff shall be appointed by the Secretary-General.

The matter might have rested there, but it was not to be as simple as that—as Lie was soon to find out. The Preparatory Commission of the United Nations devoted a good deal of attention to the organization of the Secretariat, and its proposals were approved by the General Assembly without any amendment of substance.[85] The Secretariat was to be divided into eight principal units, each to be headed by an Assistant Secretary-General. One Assistant Secretary-General was to be designated by the Secretary-General to deputize for him should he be absent or unable to perform his functions. This preparatory work facilitated Lie's task, but it meant that he did not have an entirely free hand. Indeed, he reports that the Big Five 'had agreed among themselves to ask me to appoint a national of each of them as an Assistant Secretary-General'.[86] They had also agreed that the top post in the political department should be held by a Soviet national.

Lie's first idea was to appoint to the political department A. A. Roshchin, who later served as the Soviet member of the Committee of Experts on the Secretariat. The Soviet government told Lie that Roshchin was not sufficiently experienced and offered A. A. Sobolev. The Secretary-General appointed Sobolev and found him a man of high ability. Sobolev later resigned and succeeded Andrei Vyshinsky as Soviet Permanent Representative to the United Nations; he subsequently became a Deputy Foreign Minister of the Soviet Union. The United

States wished to have a United States citizen as head of the Administrative and Financial Services and put forward the name of John B. Hutson, at that time Under-Secretary of Agriculture. Hutson was appointed and served for a short time. The United Kingdom, says Lie, 'took an approach which was so solicitous of my right to appoint whatever British subject I chose . . . as to be not quite helpful'.[87] Various names were canvassed, and in the end Lie appointed to the Economic Department David Owen, who now serves as Executive Chairman of the Technical Assistance Board. Of the French names suggested, Lie chose Henri Laugier to head the Department of Social Affairs, and for the Trusteeship Department he appointed Victor Hoo, a Chinese national, who is now Commissioner for Technical Assistance. The remaining top posts went to Benjamin A. Cohen of Chile, Ivan Kerno of Czechoslovakia, and Adrian Pelt of the Netherlands. Thus the eight senior posts were allocated on a fairly wide geographical basis: three to Western Europe, two to Eastern Europe, and one each to Asia, Latin America, and North America. The fact that, including the Secretary-General, six of the top nine posts were held by Europeans seems not to have been regarded in 1946 as inappropriate.

Inevitably there was a good deal of improvisation in the early years. Lie was often preoccupied with major political questions and left administrative matters to his colleagues. He normally held a weekly meeting with the top officials. An agenda was circulated in advance and minutes were kept, but the matters discussed tended to be relatively trivial. Lines of authority became increasingly blurred, and it was not entirely clear whether the Assistant Secretaries-General were officers in charge of departments or a panel of top-level advisors to the Secretary-General—or both.

By 1952, the time had come to review the organization of the Secretariat. Lie had evidently reached the conclusion that the organizational pattern recommended by the Preparatory

Commission and approved by the General Assembly was not entirely satisfactory, but it was not until he had decided to resign that he made public his own ideas.[88] He proposed the abandonment of the eight Assistant Secretaries-General in favor of the division of the Secretariat into three major groups of departments, each under a Deputy Secretary-General, as follows:

Deputy for Political and Public Affairs
    Political and Security Council Affairs
    Trusteeship and Information from Non-Self-Governing Territories
    Public Information
Deputy for Economic and Social Affairs
    Economic Affairs
    Social Affairs
    Technical Assistance
Deputy for Administrative and Conference Services
    Administrative and Financial Services
    Conference and General Services
    Library

Lie believed this rearrangement would lead to increased administrative efficiency, particularly in the economic and social field, and would have two other important advantages. First, it would enable the Secretary-General to devote his entire energies to the most important problems of policy by freeing him from questions of day-to-day operation, administration, and co-ordination. ('I never loved administrative details', he later wrote.[89]) Secondly, it would provide the Secretary-General with a small group of deputies of the highest competence and prestige.

Hammarskjold did not proceed with Lie's proposals for reorganization but developed his own plan. His first report on the organization of the Secretariat was submitted to the General Assembly in November 1953, and the consequent reorganization was in effect completed in February 1959 with the amalgamation of the Technical Assistance Administration with the Department of Economic and Social Affairs. Hammarskjold, unlike Lie, was interested in administrative matters and wished to bring the administrative units under his own personal supervision. He abolished the two grades of senior official in favor of one supervisory grade, with the title of Under-Secretary. He appointed Under-Secretaries in charge of the 'substantive' Departments related to the work of the three Councils as well as two Under-Secretaries without portfolio (later called Under-Secretaries for Special Political Affairs). He rearranged the other units into six offices: Legal Affairs, Controller, Personnel, Public Information, Conference Services, and General Services.

The top level of the Secretariat at Headquarters at the time of Hammarskjold's death was as follows:

Four heads of offices in the central administration of the Secretariat (Under-Secretary for General Assembly and Related Affairs, the Legal Counsel, the Controller, and the Director of Personnel).

Two Under-Secretaries for Special Political Affairs, of whom one was also *Chef de cabinet* to the Secretary-General.

Three Under-Secretaries concerned with substantive questions (Political and Security Council Affairs, Economic and Social Affairs, and Trusteeship and Information from Non-Self-Governing Territories).

One official of Under-Secretary rank, within the Department of Economic and Social Affairs, concerned with technical assistance.

Three Under-Secretaries concerned with 'servicing' departments (Public Information, Conference Services, and General Services).

Other officials of Under-Secretary rank comprised the Director of the United Nations Office in Geneva, the Executive Secre-

68

taries of the four regional economic commissions, the administrative heads of five extra-budgetary programs, one official
appointed by the Security Council (the Representative for
India and Pakistan), one official elected by the General Assembly
(the Plebiscite Commissioner for the Cameroons), and five
officials on special field missions (two in the Middle East, two
in the Congo, and one in Laos).

Hammarskjold was reluctant to 'freeze' any arrangement for the delegation of his personal responsibilities in the
event of his absence from Headquarters, ill health, or other
circumstances which might prevent him from discharging his
duties. The General Assembly had resolved during the first
part of the first session that 'There shall always be one Assistant
Secretary-General designated by the Secretary-General to
deputize for him when he is absent or unable to perform his
functions'.[90] Hammarskjold, who was often absent from
Headquarters, reported to the General Assembly in 1957 as
follows:

> The head of each department and office is directed
> to carry on his operations and to make such decisions as
> are necessary within the limits of established policy. Where
> marginal policy questions or new questions of importance
> not covered by existing policy, arise, the daily contact
> maintained by the Secretary-General through the Execu-
> tive Office provides a basis for his continuing direction of
> the Secretariat. It is only on those occasions when, due
> to unsatisfactory communications, the Secretary-General
> is both absent and unavailable, that some special measure
> would appear to be indicated. In these circumstances,
> it is my view that an arrangement should be made whereby
> a group or 'panel', consisting of the Under-Secretary
> confronted with an urgent and important policy decision,
> not covered by existing policy lines, associated with two
> other Under-Secretaries selected on the basis of geo-
> graphical distribution should make the decision.[91]

69

The Advisory Committee commented that this arrangement did not seem to be entirely in harmony with the Assembly's decision, but Hammarskjold pointed out that political conditions had changed rapidly since the resolution had been adopted in 1946 and there had been a significant development also in the Secretary-General's political functions and responsibilities. In the circumstances, he felt that the full delegation of the Secretary-General's responsibilities, especially in the political field, to one individual might rightly incur objections from Member States while a three-member panel of varying composition could keep its decisions out of the area of political conflict.[92]

Until 1960, the organization of the Secretariat was regarded as, in the main, an administrative matter, to be settled by the Secretary-General in the light of the comments of the Advisory Committee and the Assembly's Fifth Committee; political considerations had rarely been injected into the discussions. Khrushchev's proposal for a collective executive body at the head of the Secretariat was vigorously political in character, and the reactions of other governments were inevitably political. Although the proposal evoked virtually no support outside the Soviet bloc, it brought to the surface undercurrents of feeling about the organization of the Secretariat. Several of the African and Asian countries, in particular, tried to devise some compromise between the Soviet proposal and the arrangements then in force. These efforts at compromise, which were directed to the political rather than the administrative aspects of the problem, retained the idea of a single Secretary-General, but with a group of three deputies representing the three groups of States mentioned by Khrushchev. This formula came to be known as the 'sub-troika'.

President Nkrumah of Ghana seems to have been the first to put the idea forward, in a statement to the United Nations Correspondents Association on 30 September 1960. He said that the time had come for the appointment of three

Deputy Secretaries-General, acceptable to the Western and Eastern blocs and to the neutralist countries. He considered that these Deputy Secretaries-General should be invested with clearly defined authority and should not be required to act merely as assistants to the Secretary-General. In his view, the acceptance of this proposal would relieve the Office of the Secretary-General of controversy and criticism. He reiterated this view at the conference of neutral States in Belgrade in September 1961.

President Sékou Touré of Guinea advanced a similar proposal in the more formal setting of the General Assembly in 1960:

> As regards the office of the Secretary-General, we should like to make a suggestion which seems to us to go a long way towards meeting the concern of the Soviet Union, while retaining a desirable harmony at the highest executive level of the United Nations. For us, there can be no question of three Secretaries-General but only of one. What we suggest is the establishment of three posts of Assistant Secretary-General to be filled in accordance with the proposals made by the countries representing the three main political trends in the United Nations. In this way, the implementation of General Assembly resolutions would be more in keeping with political realities, since each Assistant Secretary-General, working in direct association with the Secretary-General, whose function is co-ordination, would be responsible for the geographical area which proposed him.[93]

The 'sub-troika' idea never really got off the ground in 1960, but some elements of it are to be found in the recommendations of three members of the Committee of Experts on the Secretariat (Quaison-Sackey, Loutfi, and Venkatachar). They proposed that the Secretary-General should appoint three Deputy Secretaries-General, taking into account the main political trends. These Deputies should be men of eminence and high attainments, distinguished in public affairs, and should serve for one term only.[94]

The Soviet member of the Committee of Experts put forward the full 'troika' idea, and in one respect extended it: 'The *entire staff* of the United Nations Secretariat,' he wrote, 'should be reorganized . . . so that the three main groups of States . . . are represented in it on an equal footing.'[95]

Other members of the Committee suggested that there should be a reduction in the number of top-level posts from thirteen to eight, and eventually to seven; these officials would act as the advisers of the Secretary-General.[96]

Hammarskjold himself was evidently in favor of maintaining the number of top-echelon officials at about thirteen or fourteen, but he proposed that five of them, selected on a broad regional basis, should be responsible for advising the Secretary-General on political problems. One would be a United States citizen, one a Soviet citizen, and three would be from countries outside any power bloc.[97]

There is, of course, no magic in any particular number of officials suggested for the top echelon. If the problem were solely administrative in character, the most convenient course would no doubt be to establish one senior level of official immediately below the Secretary-General and allocate the work to Secretariat units, necessarily differing in size and importance, each under a senior official. In addition, it would be desirable to have available for *ad hoc* assignments a number of highly qualified top-level officials without major departmental responsibilities, who could undertake important field duties on an emergency basis.

But administrative convenience is not the only consideration. The organizational arrangements at the top level must pay regard to the importance of wide geographical distribution, taking account also of two other facts: that geographical regions are unequal in size, and that there are important political and ideological differences within the regions. Finally, any arrangement must necessarily be within the framework of existing staff contracts.

Implicit in all the plans current at the time of Hammarskjold's death was the notion that there should be a more formalized and representative system of top-level consultation in the Secretariat. Too high a proportion of top-echelon officials, it was felt, were citizens of Western countries. Indeed, one high official of United States nationality, Andrew W. Cordier, who had served as Executive Assistant to both Lie and Hammarskjold, had intimated that he would resign specifically 'in order to assist in the adjustment of posts at the Under-Secretary level, taking into account the much enlarged and revised geographical character of the membership of the United Nations'.[98]

In the private discussions that preceded the appointment of U Thant, much attention was devoted to the distribution of top posts and the responsibilities which should attach to them. The starting point seems to have been the idea of five top-echelon officials with political responsibilities, which had been favored by the three past Presidents of the General Assembly and by Hammarskjold.[99] When it was realized that none of the five top political officials would be from western Europe, it was suggested by several west European Member States that the number might be increased from five to six. The Soviet Union promptly countered with a proposal of seven, to include a Soviet citizen and also a citizen of another country of the Soviet bloc. The argument was ended when U Thant let it be known that he was prepared to decide the question of top posts on his own responsibility in the light of a statement he would make after his appointment. This statement, together with subsequent announcements, set out the following arrangement.[100]

(1) U Thant designated eight principal advisers, selected on a wide geographical basis. They are members of the

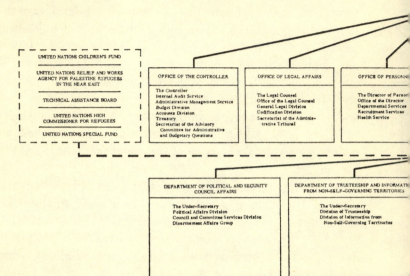

UNITED NATIONS CHILDREN'S FUND

UNITED NATIONS RELIEF AND WORKS AGENCY FOR PALESTINE REFUGEES IN THE NEAR EAST

TECHNICAL ASSISTANCE BOARD

UNITED NATIONS HIGH COMMISSIONER FOR REFUGEES

UNITED NATIONS SPECIAL FUND

OFFICE OF THE CONTROLLER

The Controller
Internal Audit Service
Administrative Management Service
Budget Division
Accounts Division
Treasury
Secretariat of the Advisory
 Committee for Administrative
 and Budgetary Questions

OFFICE OF LEGAL AFFAIRS

The Legal Counsel
Office of the Legal Counsel
General Legal Division
Codification Division
Secretariat of the Adminis-
 trative Tribunal

OFFICE OF PERSONNE

The Director of Personn
Office of the Director
Departmental Services
Recruitment Services
Health Service

DEPARTMENT OF POLITICAL AND SECURITY COUNCIL AFFAIRS

The Under-Secretary
Political Affairs Division
Council and Committee Services Division
Disarmament Affairs Group

DEPARTMENT OF TRUSTEESHIP AND INFORMATI FROM NON-SELF-GOVERNING TERRITORIES

The Under-Secretary
Division of Trusteeship
Division of Information from
 Non-Self-Governing Territories

OFFICE OF CONFERENCE SERVICES

The Under-Secretary
Language and Meetings Service
Publishing Service
Stenographic Service
 (English, French, Russian and Spanish sections)
Library

OF

The U
Econo
Press,
Divisi
Divisi
Inform

INF

ACCRA
ADDIS ABABA
ASUNCION
ATHENS
BAGHDAD
BANGKOK
BEIRUT
BELGRADE
BOGOTA
BUENOS AIRES
CAIRO

Forms part of the UN Office at Geneva.

74

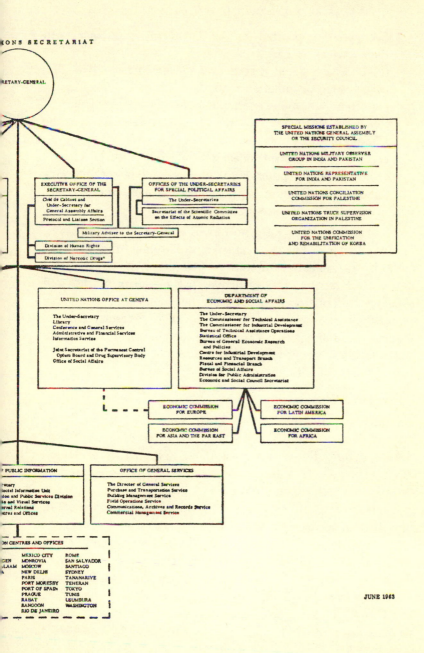

KONS SECRETARIAT

SECRETARY-GENERAL

SPECIAL MISSIONS ESTABLISHED BY THE UNITED NATIONS GENERAL ASSEMBLY OR THE SECURITY COUNCIL

UNITED NATIONS MILITARY OBSERVER GROUP IN INDIA AND PAKISTAN

UNITED NATIONS REPRESENTATIVE FOR INDIA AND PAKISTAN

UNITED NATIONS CONCILIATION COMMISSION FOR PALESTINE

UNITED NATIONS TRUCE SUPERVISION ORGANIZATION IN PALESTINE

UNITED NATIONS COMMISSION FOR THE UNIFICATION AND REHABILITATION OF KOREA

EXECUTIVE OFFICE OF THE SECRETARY-GENERAL

Chef de Cabinet and Under-Secretary for General Assembly Affairs
Protocol and Liaison Section

OFFICES OF THE UNDER-SECRETARIES FOR SPECIAL POLITICAL AFFAIRS

The Under-Secretaries

Secretariat of the Scientific Committee on the Effects of Atomic Radiation

Military Adviser to the Secretary-General

Division of Human Rights

Division of Narcotic Drugs*

UNITED NATIONS OFFICE AT GENEVA

The Under-Secretary
Library
Conference and General Services
Administrative and Financial Services
Information Service

Joint Secretariat of the Permanent Central Opium Board and Drug Supervisory Body
Office of Social Affairs

DEPARTMENT OF ECONOMIC AND SOCIAL AFFAIRS

The Under-Secretary
The Commissioner for Technical Assistance
The Commissioner for Industrial Development
Bureau of Technical Assistance Operations
Statistical Office
Bureau of General Economic Research and Policies
Centre for Industrial Development
Resources and Transport Branch
Fiscal and Financial Branch
Bureau of Social Affairs
Division for Public Administration
Economic and Social Council Secretariat

ECONOMIC COMMISSION FOR EUROPE

ECONOMIC COMMISSION FOR LATIN AMERICA

ECONOMIC COMMISSION FOR ASIA AND THE FAR EAST

ECONOMIC COMMISSION FOR AFRICA

PUBLIC INFORMATION

retary
Social Information Unit
ion and Public Services Division
s and Visual Services
rnal Relations
tres and Offices

OFFICE OF GENERAL SERVICES

The Director of General Services
Purchase and Transportation Service
Building Management Service
Field Operations Service
Communications, Archives and Records Service
Commercial Management Service

ON CENTRES AND OFFICES

GEN	MEXICO CITY	ROME
LAAM	MONROVIA	SAN SALVADOR
A	MOSCOW	SANTIAGO
	NEW DELHI	SYDNEY
	PARIS	TANANARIVE
	PORT MORESBY	TEHERAN
	PORT OF SPAIN	TOKYO
	PRAGUE	TUNIS
	RABAT	USUMBURA
	RANGOON	WASHINGTON
	RIO DE JANEIRO	

JUNE 1963

7 5

Secretariat, appointed by U Thant in accordance with the Charter.

(2) U Thant stated that he will consult them individually, collectively, or otherwise, as the occasion demands, on important questions pertaining to the performance of functions entrusted to the Secretary-General by the Charter.

(3) The arrangement does not interfere with U Thant's right to consult other high officials, and is without prejudice to such future organizational changes as experience may reveal to be necessary.

There has thus been no formal erosion of the provisions of the Charter. The Secretary-General retains the exclusive authority to appoint staff and to determine the organization of the Secretariat. The principle that members of the staff should be international officials, and not regional or ideological representatives, remains unimpaired. The Secretary-General consults his colleagues, at his discretion, in whatever manner seems to him appropriate; and this does not derogate from his responsibilities under the Charter.

Geographical Distribution

An international organization should be staffed on an international basis. This is not simply a matter of equity; it is necessary for effective administration. No nation or region has a monopoly of human wisdom. The Secretariat needs a diversity of cultures, traditions, and beliefs. Fifty years ago it might have been necessary to justify the principle of an international secretariat; today we may take it for granted.

This is not to say that posts should be allocated among Member States on an equal or any other mechanical basis. There is no sanction in the Charter for the idea that countries or regions have a right to a quota of posts. What is stated in the Charter is that the Secretariat has an exclusively international character. The aim is to obtain the highest standards

of performance and integrity, and at the same time to ensure
that the Secretariat is 'enriched by the experience and culture
which each Member nation can furnish' and that each Member
State should be satisfied that 'its own culture and philosophy
make a full contribution to the Secretariat'.[101]

Article 101 (3) of the Charter seeks to establish priorities.
The first sentence states what shall be the paramount consideration in the employment of the staff and in the determination of the conditions of service. It shall be the necessity of
securing the highest standards of efficiency, competence, and
integrity. The second sentence deals not with the paramount
consideration, but with a matter to the importance of which
due regard shall be paid, namely, recruiting the staff on as
wide a geographical basis as possible. To the plain man,
Article 101 (3) admits of no ambiguity.

But to assert that the wording of the Charter is not
ambiguous does not mean that problems may not arise in
practice. It is, after all, at least theoretically conceivable that
it might be difficult to recruit, on a wide geographical basis, all
staff of the required standards. This is true, for example, of
posts with special linguistic requirements. On the other hand,
there may be circumstances in which there is a geographical
element in 'efficiency' or 'competence'. For reasons of sound
administration, and without reference to geographical distribution, it may be desirable that a high proportion of the staff
of a regional commission should come from the region concerned.

It was inevitable, in the early days, that staff should be
recruited from those of the original Member States which were
best able to release qualified personnel. In 1946, two-thirds
of the internationally-recruited staff at United Nations Headquarters were citizens of the United States, the United Kingdom, or France. The initial imbalance has been slowly modified
over the years by recruiting on a wide geographical basis.
The percentage of North Americans has been halved, and

there have been significant increases for all other regions except Europe.

TABLE 3

Professional staff, percentage by regions, 1946 and 1963[102]

	1946 %	1963 %
Western Europe	32	26
Eastern Europe	7	12
Middle East	less than one	4
Africa	less than one	8
Asia and the Far East	7	18
Latin America	4	10
North America and the Caribbean	50	22

N.B. The 1946 figures are for 'internationally recruited staff at Headquarters'; the 1963 figures are for 'staff in professional and higher level posts subject to geographical distribution'.

While the slow process of extending the geographical distribution of staff has been taking place, membership of the United Nations has increased from the original figure of fifty-one States to more than one hundred. Most of the new Member States have only recently acquired independence. Their representatives, having witnessed the disappearance of the colonial system at home, find that many members of the United Nations Secretariat at Headquarters are from western countries. An understandable reaction is to urge that the imbalance be corrected as promptly as possible.

It is, of course, easier to complain that things are unsatisfactory than to suggest remedies. There are several reasons why progress has been and will be slow. First, in any one year there are less than two hundred new appointments. Two-thirds of these are likely to be short-service staff from Eastern Europe, the Middle East, Africa, Asia, and Latin America. In other words, two-thirds of the vacancies in any one year will be used to replace temporary staff from regions which have generally been regarded as 'under-represented' in the Secretariat, and not to change the over-all balance.

Secondly, there is a world-wide shortage of persons with the necessary technical and linguistic skills and who are by temperament qualified for service with international agencies. The Director of Personnel reported a few years ago that in one country, whose representative had just spoken on the question of geographical distribution, ten or twelve excellent candidates for United Nations posts had been found by the Secretary-General's representative but none had been available to accept appointment.[103]

Thirdly, governments have not always cooperated as fully as they might have done with the Office of Personnel in the search for qualified staff. I refer below to some of the difficulties encountered in this regard.

The International Civil Service Advisory Board has warned against a strict quota system for appointments. 'The Board is aware that various bases for a quota system have been advanced but it has the firm conviction that the fixing of any rigid quota for geographical distribution would be extremely harmful. . . .'[104] In practice, the quota idea makes a strong appeal. It should, however, be emphasized that any formula tends to elevate arithmetic above common sense. Geographical distribution is necessarily based on the *present* nationality or citizenship of each staff member, whatever his or her country of origin. The countries of the Soviet bloc have objected that some Secretariat posts are filled by 'persons who had left their homeland many years before' and 'displayed a hostile attitude towards their own country', and have complained that the Secretariat decides on its own initiative 'which staff members could be placed on the quota of a particular Member State. . . .'[105] They hold that 'only the country concerned can decide who is or is not its citizen and who can or cannot represent it in the Secretariat'.[106]

During the second session of the General Assembly, Colombia proposed that geographical distribution within the Secretariat should be based on quotas related to the financial contribution of each Member. This proposal was rejected by 20 votes to 19, with 7 abstentions.[107] Shortly afterward, however, Secretary-General Lie concluded that although any rigid mathematical formula for geographical distribution was unacceptable, a flexible system could be based on financial contributions to the United Nations budget not because wealth should be the determining factor but because budgetary assessments had been fixed in relation to a combination of relevant criteria. In order to allow reasonable flexibility, he proposed to allow an upward or downward variation within 25 per cent of the budgetary assessment, except that there would be no upward variation in respect of countries contributing more than 10 per cent of the United Nations budget. He also decided that no country should be regarded as over-represented if the number of its nationals employed in the Secretariat was less than four. Posts with special language requirements were excluded.[108] This was the origin of the 'desirable range', which became the accepted standard by which to judge geographical distribution.

For a decade there seemed to be general satisfaction with the method of computing the 'desirable range'. Some Member States, it is true, disliked the idea of anything remotely resembling a quota system, but recognized that the 'desirable range' procedure provided, in practice, a flexible means of guiding the Secretary-General. But as the number of Members with low budgetary assessments increased, the system was criticized as being at variance with the Charter, which is based on the equality of Members without reference to material resources. The original method of computing the 'desirable range', it was held, tended to give a preponderant influence in the Secretariat to wealthy countries.

The matter was considered in 1961 by the Committee

of Experts on the Secretariat, and the majority of members favored a new formula which would recognize four factors:

(1) The membership, as such, of the Organization;
(2) The population factor;
(3) The desirability of securing over-all balance for the main geographical regions;
(4) The size of each Member State's contribution to the regular budget of the United Nations.[109]

This formula seems to have originated with the Soviet expert, A. A. Roshchin,[110] who later filed a separate statement making a quite different proposal. It is not unreasonable to deduce from the other separate statements appended to the report of the Committee that the proposed formula was accepted by some members of the Committee as a compromise, on the assumption that all members of the Committee supported it. If the other members of the Committee had known or foreseen that Roshchin would file a dissenting report, they might not have been so willing to accept a compromise.

When the question of geographical distribution came before the General Assembly's Fifth Committee in 1961, there was a strong disposition to give a good deal of weight in any new formula to the principle of the equality of United Nations Members. Venezuela suggested that 'each Member State, whether large or small, rich or poor, should be assigned a substantial minimum number of posts—say ten'; this was supported by Burma. Ceylon favoured the idea that Secretariat posts should be distributed among Member States on an equal basis. Iraq, the Philippines, and Nigeria were among those speaking in favour of a minimum allocation to each Member State of about five posts.[111]

Two draft resolutions were submitted to the Fifth Committee, though neither was put to the vote. One, in its final revision, referred to 'at least four nationals of each Member State'; the other referred to a 'target of a minimum of five staff members from each Member State'. Both would have introduced a population factor, and both would have continued to take account of financial contributions.[112]

The Fifth Committee was, however, unable to reach a consensus, and no resolution was adopted. The Assembly decided, however, to invite the Secretary-General to 'take into consideration the contents of the two draft resolutions and also the views expressed in the Committee' and to present to the session of the General Assembly in 1962 'his considered views on how to improve the geographical distribution of the staff. . . .'[113]

The Secretary-General's proposal was as follows. In the Secretariat proper, for professional posts other than those with special language requirements, an equitable geographical distribution would take account of the fact of membership, of Members' contributions, and of their populations. An appropriate allocation to each of these factors for the time being might be (i) a minimum range of one to five posts attributable to membership; (ii) a reservation of one hundred posts to take account of such differences in size of population as do not receive sufficient weight in the other two factors; and (iii) the balance of posts to be assigned on the basis of the ratios of assessed contributions: in a staff of 1,500 this factor would amount to some 60 per cent.[114] This was approved by the General Assembly in 1962, with the specific stipulation that 'no Member State should be considered "over-represented" if it has no more than five of its nationals on the staff by virtue of its membership'. The Assembly recommended that the Secretary-General should also take account of the relative importance of posts at different levels and the need for a more balanced regional composition of the staff at levels of D-1 and above; and that in making career appointments, particular account should be taken of the need to reduce 'under-representation'.[115] The Secretary-General, in reporting in 1963 on the effects of the changes, insisted that arithmetical terms should not be a substitute for discretion and good sense. He intended to treat the new statistical formula 'as a sign-post' toward the accomplishment of a more balanced composition.[116]

The new formula had some curious consequences. For about half the Member States, the 'desirable range' in 1963 was 2—5. For a few States, however, the range was from a higher figure to a lower, and in three cases the formula gave no flexibility at all. The 'desirable range' for Spain, for example, was 12—12; for both Brazil and Czechoslovakia it was 14—14.

The effect of the new method of calculation was to increase the 'desirable range' for the Afro-Asian area and Latin America, and to reduce it for both Eastern and Western Europe, and for North America and the Caribbean. Table 4 gives the mid-point of the 'desirable range', by regions, for 1948, 1962, and 1963. The figures for 1948 and 1962 are based on budgetary assessments only; the 1963 figures also take account of the fact of membership and members' populations.

TABLE 4

Mid-point of 'Desirable Range', by Regions[117]

	1948 'desirable range'		1962 'desirable range'		1963 'desirable range'	
	median	percentage	median	percentage	median	percentage
Western Europe	228	23·5	350	23·1	294	19·6
Eastern Europe	97	10·0	300	19·8	263	17·5
Middle East	26	2·7	28	1·9	53	3·6
Asia and the Far East	132	13·6	204	13·5	246	16·3
Africa	23	2·4	68	4·5	136	9·1
Latin America	84	8·6	88	5·8	121	8·1
North America and the Caribbean	381	39·2	476	31·4	387	25·8

I now examine each region.

Western Europe. Staff from Western Europe totalled 295 in 1947. The 'desirable range' in 1963 was 312–275, and there were 349 staff members from Member States, together with 22 staff members from non-Member States. There has been some variation within the region; the six States admitted to the Organization in 1955, which had only 10 nationals in the Secretariat in 1956, had a total of 65 in 1963.

Eastern Europe. At the time of the Secretary-General's report in 1948, Eastern Europe had 72 staff members, as against a 'desirable range' of 73–120. As the Secretariat grew in size and the number of Member States from the region increased, the 'desirable range' for Eastern Europe had increased to 289–236 in 1963. The number of staff members in 1963 was 164, of whom 134 were on short-term appointments. Albania had no nationals in the Secretariat.

Virtually all the staff now recruited from Eastern Europe are for temporary appointments, so that considerable effort is needed simply to maintain the number of East Europeans in the Secretariat. Moreover, the countries of the Soviet bloc are opposed to the principle of career appointments, even for nationals from other regions.

TABLE 5

Appointments from Eastern Europe to posts subject to
geographical distribution, 1955–1963

Year	Career appointments	Short-service appointments
1955–1956	2	9
1956–1957	–	12
1957–1958	–	11
1958–1959	–	10
1959–1960	2	28
1960–1961	–	42
1961–1962	–	48
1962–1963	–	32

Middle East. Staff from the Middle East increased from 7

in 1947 to 60 in 1963, when the 'desirable range' for the region was 35–72. All States in the region except Kuwait and Yemen had staff in the Secretariat in 1963.

Asia and the Far East. This region, which includes Australia and New Zealand, had 62 staff members in 1947, 32 of them Chinese. The 'desirable range' in 1963 was 243–248, and there were 241 staff members from Member States, together with 3 from non-Member States.

Africa. Before the admission of sixteen new African States in 1960, Africa was slightly in excess of the top figure of the 'desirable range'. With 105 staff members in 1963, Africa as a region was within the 'desirable range' of 86–187, but there were nine African States without nationals in the Secretariat.

Latin America. Latin Americans in the Secretariat doubled in numbers between 1947 and 1961. The 1963 total was 140, with a 'desirable range' of 96–147. Only Nicaragua had no nationals in the Secretariat.

North America and the Caribbean. Staff members from North America (Canada, the United States) and the Caribbean (Jamaica, Trinidad and Tobago) totalled 299 in 1963, against a 'desirable range' of 457–317.

TABLE 6

Regional distribution of staff subject to geographical distribution, 31 August 1963[118]

Region	No. of U.N. members	Budgetary assessments 1964	Number of staff			'Desirable range'
			Short-service	Career	Total	
Western Europe	16	22·60	57	292	349*	312–275
Eastern Europe	10	21·24	134	30	164	289–236
Middle East	12	1·22	20	40	60	35–72
Asia and the Far East	16	12·82	71	170	241	243–248
Africa	33	2·49	53	52	105	86–187
Latin America	20	4·73	42	98	140	96–147
North America and the Caribbean	4	35·23	32	267	299	457–317

* Figures include 10 staff members from non-self-governing territories, 4 of them from Africa, 2 from Asia, and 4 from the Caribbean area.

TABLE 7

Staff, by nationality, 31 August 1963[119]

	Staff subject to geographical distribution			'Desirable range'	Posts with special language requirements	Staff specifically appointed for mission service
	short-term	career	total			
Afghanistan	–	3	3	2–5	—	—
Albania	–	—	—	2–5	—	—
Algeria	–	—	—	2–6	—	—
Argentina	7	13	20	14–13	24	3
Australia	3	12	15	22–19	3	1
Austria	1	8	9	7–9	—	2
Belgium	2	17	19	16–15	6	—
Bolivia	3	3	6	2–5	1	—
Brazil	8	12	20	14–14	—	2
Bulgaria	6	1	7	4–7	—	—
Burma	5	3	8	2–6	—	—
Burundi	–	—	—	2–5	—	—
Byelorussian S.S.R.	2	—	2	8–9	2	—
Cambodia	–	2	2	2–5	—	—
Cameroon	1	1	2	2–5	—	—
Canada	5	27	32	41–31	4	9
Central African Republic	–	—	—	2–5	—	—
Ceylon	3	6	9	2–6	—	1
Chad	–	—	—	2–5	—	—
Chile	2	16	18	4–7	7	1
China	2	45	47	59–43	53	—
Colombia	4	9	13	4–7	3	—
Congo (Brazza-ville)	–	—	—	2–5	—	—
Congo (Leopold-ville)	1	1	2	2–6	—	—
Costa Rica	–	3	3	2–5	1	—
Cuba	1	5	6	4–7	1	—
Cyprus	2	—	2	2–5	—	—
Czechoslovakia	17	4	21	14–14	—	—
Dahomey	3	—	3	2–5	—	—
Denmark	–	9	9	8–10	—	3
Dominican Republic	–	2	2	2–5	2	—
Ecuador	2	6	8	2–5	1	—
El Salvador	2	1	3	2–5	—	—
Ethopia	3	7	10	2–5	—	—
Federation of Malaya	–	2	2	3–6	—	—
Finland	–	6	6	6–8	1	—
France	12	67	79	77–55	116	9
Gabon	1	—	1	2–5	—	—
Ghana	5	3	8	2–6	—	1

TABLE 7—*cont.*

| | Staff subject to geographical distribution | | | 'Desirable range' | Posts with special language requirements | Staff specifically appointed for mission service |
	short-term	career	total			
Greece	5	4	9	4–7	—	3
Guatemala	1	1	2	2–5	—	—
Guinea	—	—	—	2–5	—	—
Haiti	—	4	4	2–5	—	6
Honduras	1	1	2	2–5	—	—
Hungary	7	2	9	7–9	—	—
Iceland	—	1	1	2–5	—	—
India	18	48	66	27–22	—	4
Indonesia	5	6	11	7–9	—	—
Iran	2	6	8	4–7	—	—
Iraq	2	3	5	2–6	1	—
Ireland	2	3	5	3–6	2	2
Israel	3	3	6	3–6	3	1
Italy	9	18	27	29–24	2	5
Ivory Coast	—	—	—	2–5	—	—
Jamaica	5	1	6	2–5	—	—
Japan	12	14	26	30–24	—	—
Jordan	2	6	8	2–5	—	1
Kuwait	—	—	—	2–5	—	—
Laos	1	1	2	2–5	—	—
Lebanon	3	5	8	2–5	2	5
Liberia	2	1	3	2–5	—	—
Libya	1	—	1	2–5	—	—
Luxembourg	—	2	2	2–5	—	1
Madagascar	2	—	2	2–5	—	—
Mali	1	—	1	2–5	—	—
Mauritania	—	—	—	2–5	—	—
Mexico	6	7	13	10–11	4	—
Mongolia	1	—	1	2–5	—	—
Morocco	—	—	2	3–6	2	—
Nepal	1	4	5	2–5	—	—
Netherlands	3	19	22	14–13	—	5
New Zealand	5	6	11	6–8	—	4
Nicaragua	—	—	—	2–5	—	—
Niger	—	—	—	2–5	—	—
Nigeria	4	4	8	4–7	—	—
Norway	1	12	13	7–9	—	2
Pakistan	6	9	15	6–9	—	1
Panama	—	2	2	2–5	—	—
Paraguay	—	3	3	2–5	1	—
Peru	2	4	6	2–6	3	—
Philippines	7	7	14	6–8	—	—
Poland	10	16	26	17–16	1	—
Portugal	—	—	2	3–6	—	—
Romania	3	—	3	5–8	—	—
Rwanda	1	—	1	2–5	—	—
Saudi Arabia	—	—	2	2–6	—	—
Senegal	2	—	2	2–5	—	—

TABLE 7—*cont.*

	Staff subject to geographical distribution			'Desirable range'	Posts with special language requirements	Staff specifically appointed for mission service
	short-term	career	total			
Sierra Leone	1	—	1	2–5	—	—
Somalia	2	—	2	2–5	—	—
South Africa	2	13	15	8–9	—	1
Spain	3	13	16	12–12	29	2
Sudan	5	2	7	2–6	—	—
Sweden	4	11	15	18–16	—	5
Syria	1	6	7	2–5	1	—
Tanganyika	2	—	2	2–5	—	—
Thailand	2	5	7	3–6	—	—
Togo	2	2	4	2–5	—	—
Trinidad and Tobago	3	3	6	2–5	—	1
Tunisia	2	3	5	2–5	—	—
Turkey	5	6	11	6–8	—	—
Uganda	1	—	1	2–5	—	—
Ukrainian S.S.R.	10	—	10	26–22	3	—
Union of Soviet Socialist Republics	76	1	77	193–131	45	1
United Arab Republic	9	12	21	4–7	1	5
United Kingdom	15	100	115*	98–69	69	21
United States	19	236	255	412–276	80	10
Upper Volta	–	1	1	2–5	—	—
Uruguay	1	5	6	2–6	1	—
Venezuela	2	1	3	8–9	—	—
Yemen	–	–	–	2–5	—	—
Yugoslavia	3	6	9	6–8	—	2

* Includes 10 staff members from non-self-governing territories.

There have been a number of proposals for paying regard not only to the geographical distribution of posts, but also to the relative importance of posts at various levels. The justification for proposals of this kind, as explained by the Committee of Experts on the Secretariat, is that 'an otherwise adequate number of posts at junior levels does not compensate for the absence of staff at senior levels'.[120] UNESCO used a system of weighting from 1949 until 1960; the Food and Agriculture Organization adopted a weighting system in 1957.

The main argument against weighting posts at various levels is that everything possible should be done to minimize the nationality element in the promotion process. Wide geographical distribution can properly be applied to recruiting, but promotion should be based on merit.

> Both the efficiency of the organization and the morale of the staff will suffer serious damage if considerations of competence and reasonable career opportunities are not much more heavily weighted in promotions than is the factor of balance of nationalities throughout the Secretariat.[121]

The Secretary-General reviewed this question in 1962 but came to the conclusion that if a system based on salary levels were introduced, the picture of the geographical distribution of the staff would be changed only slightly from the picture given by counting each post equally. He doubted whether the differences were sufficiently meaningful to justify the additional complexities which the weighting of posts would bring to any formula.[122] The Assembly did not recommend that the new formula should take account of the relative importance of posts, but the need for a more balanced regional composition at levels of D–1 and above was noted.[123] The Secretary-General reported in 1963 that regional readjustment at the D–1 level should not be expected too quickly. There should be no impairment of the reasonable expectations of staff members for promotion; imbalance should be corrected by the careful use of fixed-term appointments at higher levels.[124]

For a time there was some doubt whether some 160 Headquarters posts in the principal level of the General Service category should come within the scope of geographical distribution. There has always been general agreement that geographical distribution should apply to professional and higher-level posts (P–1 and above), other than posts with special language requirements. There has also been agreement that it should not cover posts subject to local recruitment. The staff rules were inconsistent, however, since they provided:

(*a*) that General Service staff would normally be regarded as locally recruited;

and (*b*) that recruitment on as wide a geographical basis as possible would not apply to General Service posts, *except the principal level of that category at Headquarters.*

In his report on geographical distribution in 1960, the Secretary-General omitted G–5 staff on the ground that recruitment at that level 'is not made on an international basis'.[125] There was disagreement within the Fifth Committee on whether G–5 staff should or should not come within the scope of geographical distribution, and the Committee of Experts on the Secretariat was asked to 'study the category of posts subject to geographical distribution'.[126] The Committee of Experts did not make a definitive recommendation but suggested that, for the time being, G–5 posts *should* be subject to geographical distribution. Hammarskjold commented that such a course 'would appear to be inconsistent with the principles on which recruitment for this category is based'.[127]

The matter was not resolved in 1961, and the Secretary-General accordingly reported on the situation in 1962. But he suggested that 'the balance of advantage would lie in excluding G–5 Staff at Headquarters from any formula of geographical distribution'.[128] The matter was again considered in the Fifth Committee, which rejected a proposal to apply geographical distribution to G–5 Staff at Headquarters.[129] Staff Rule 104.5 was accordingly revised to read as follows:

Recruitment on as wide a geographical basis as possible, in accordance with the requirements of Staff Regulation 4.2, shall not apply to posts in the General Service category or in similar salary levels.

Pressure to bring G–5 staff within the scope of geographical distribution has now largely disappeared, though the matter was raised in 1963 by the representatives of the Soviet Union, Romania, and Nigeria.[130]

The suggestion has been made from time to time that the scope of geographical distribution should be extended to the staff of the extra-budgetary programs. The Committee of Experts on the Secretariat considered that the administrative staff of the Technical Assistance Board and the Special Fund 'should be included in the total United Nations staff for geographical distribution purposes'.[131] The Soviet expert would have gone further and applied geographical distribution to additional categories, including the staff of UNICEF and the High Commissioner for Refugees.[132]

The staff of the Technical Assistance Board and the Special Fund are appointed by the United Nations Director of Personnel and the activities of the two programs are intimately related to the United Nations Department of Economic and Social Affairs. There are, however, other factors which distinguish the programs from regular United Nations activities:

(a) They are financed outside the regular budget by voluntary contributions, and some non-Member States are important contributors;

TABLE 8

Staff of voluntary programs, by regions, 31 August 1963[135]

	Technical Assistance Board/ Special Fund	UNICEF
Western Europe	71	58
Eastern Europe	9	8
Middle East	9	3
Asia and the Far East	33	18
Africa	6	4
Latin America	21	10
North America and the Caribbean	42	48
	191	149
Non-Member States	14	12
	205	161

(b) They have their own governing bodies;

(c) The Technical Assistance Board is an inter-agency organ, and any proposal to apply a particular formula for geographical distribution of staff would concern all the agencies. In any case, any formula for geographical distribution would presumably have to take account of the actual contributions of States to the programs rather than their assessments under the regular budget.

U Thant reported to the Assembly in 1962 his belief 'that it would be in the interest of these programs to avoid binding them to a rigid formula even on the basis of contributions'.[133] The Assembly accepted the Secretary-General's advice, and asked him 'to review periodically the geographical distribution of the staffs of the Technical Assistance Board, the Special Fund and the United Nations Children's Fund and to report annually to the General Assembly. . . .'[134] In accordance with this request, the Secretary-General reported in 1963 on the distribution of the staffs of the programs.

As regards the experts serving under the Technical Assistance Programs, no rigid formula for geographical distri-

TABLE 9

Nationality of experts serving under the UN
technical assistance programs, 1962[137]

Region	Expanded Program	Regular Program
Western Europe	1,336	638
Eastern Europe	174	48
Middle East	75	63
Asia and the Far East	327	167
Africa	80	43
Latin America	201	138
North America and the Caribbean	348	217
Total	2,541	1,314

Note: The regions are those used in the Secretary-General's reports on geographical distribution in the Secretariat.

bution can be applied because the final choice of expert personnel lies with the recipient country. The countries of the Soviet bloc have complained that their experts are 'virtually excluded' from participation in the program,[136] but considerable progress has been made in recent years in extending the range of nationalities of United Nations experts.

The question of geographical distribution is not primarily a question of numbers but of attitude. There will always be anomalies; no formula can prevent this. Even if the Charter had stipulated that recruiting staffs on a wide geographical basis should be a paramount consideration, the problems would not be significantly different from those at present encountered. With a dynamic recruiting policy, and given the active cooperation of Member States, it should be possible within a few years to bring virtually each of the present Member States within its 'desirable range', simply by appointing nationals of 'under-represented' countries to vacancies that occur each year because of retirement, completion of contract, or other normal means. Moreover, we are entering a period when there will be a relatively large number of retirements of fairly high-level staff from Western countries. These are the officials who, when they joined the Secretariat in 1946 or 1947, were in their early forties.

It is important that personnel policy should be implemented in such a way as not to interfere with the rights of existing staff. The Committee of Experts on the Secretariat urged that consideration be given to a plan whereby 'a certain number of senior staff officers would be willing to accept early retirement, thus creating vacancies . . .' and suggested that some 'voluntary retirements . . . might take place from age of fifty'. The Committee recognized that these proposals 'might tend to impede the development of an international career service' because the recruitment of a substantial number of senior officials from outside inevitably blocks the promotion of existing career staff. The Committee suggested that this difficulty could be met by 'a temporary increase in the number of higher posts'.[138]

These proposals seem to me to involve a high price for relatively minor advantages.

In order to maintain the concept of an international career service, two conditions are necessary. First, merit should be the main criterion for appointment and an important factor in promotion.* Secondly, no contracts should be terminated solely in order to create vacancies. The Preparatory Commission considered it essential that the bulk of the staff should consist of persons making their career in the Secretariat, and that an appointment should not be terminated to make way for the appointment of a person of some other nationality or for other reasons not connected with the staff member's own work.[139]

The situation regarding geographical distribution has improved greatly in the past eight years. Lists of vacancies are circulated at regular intervals to the governments of Member States with few or no nationals in the Secretariat; discussions are held between the Secretariat and representatives of Member States; senior staff members undertake special recruitment visits to 'under-represented' countries.

But the problem for the Secretary-General and the Office of Personnel is not simply to discover qualified personnel; it is to persuade suitable persons to accept appointments. The Secretary-General has, on more than one occasion, expressed disappointment at the small response to his requests to governments for the nomination of candidates.[140] Indeed, one has some sympathy for the Secretary-General and his representatives who, year by year, listen to speakers in the Fifth Committee complaining that this or that country or region is 'under-represented' in the Secretariat, without suggesting how the situation might be changed. Moreover, it should be remembered that the Secretary-General is occasionally under pressure

* Length of service may also be a factor in promotion.

not to apply the principle of geographical distribution to particular operations, but to give preference to persons from countries which, for geographical or ideological reasons, have a special interest in the operation.*

Recruiting

The most significant difference between the League provisions for recruiting and those of the United Nations lies in the authority to appoint staff. League officials were appointed by the Secretary-General but only 'with the approval of the Council'.[141] Two staff committees advised the Secretary-General on appointments, promotions, and discharges. The role of the League Council was, in practice, a formal one, and the recommendations of the Secretary-General were normally approved without discussion.

The Secretary-General of the United Nations, by contrast, has exclusive authority in the matter of appointments. This is explicitly stated in Article 101 (1) of the Charter, and has been reaffirmed in the Staff Regulations in the following terms:

> As stated in Article 101 of the Charter, the power of appointment of staff members rests with the Secretary-General. Upon appointment each staff member shall receive a letter of appointment . . . signed by the Secretary-General or by an official in the name of the Secretary-General.[142]

The General Assembly is required by the Charter to establish 'regulations' for the appointment of staff; an International Civil Service Advisory Board is responsible, among other functions, for advice on recruitment and personnel administration for the United Nations and the specialized

* I have in mind, for example, the fact that the United Nations Information Centres in Moscow and Prague are staffed solely by citizens of the host country; also President Nkrumah's proposals for an exclusively African operation in the Congo.

agencies, and for encouraging co-ordination in conditions of service.[143] The Board's first report, issued in 1950, was concerned with recruitment methods and standards for the United Nations and the specialized agencies. An Appointment and Promotion Board, consisting of senior officials appointed by the Secretary-General, advises on the appointment, promotion, and review of staff.

The theoretically ideal method of recruitment, if merit is to be the sole criterion, would combine 'paper' qualifications, objective written examination, and personal interview of the best qualified candidates. This was never wholly achieved by the League of Nations and for three reasons. First, merit was not necessarily the only criterion for appointment. Secondly, national systems of education differed so much that it was difficult to devise forms of written examination that could be universally applied. Thirdly, ordinary methods of selection could not be wholly applicable in the case of highly technical posts or posts that had to be filled at short notice.

The chief value of including a system of open competitive examinations in the selection procedures is that it provides some protection against external pressures for the appointment of unqualified persons. Chester Purves has written of the League experience:

> The examination system . . . became not so much a method of discovering the best recruits as, in the main, a protection for the appointing authority against the importunity of delegates from countries where nepotism is still practised openly and without shame.[144]

Examinations alone can never be a sufficient basis for appointment; an examination is merely a filter that eliminates some of those who offer themselves or whose candidatures are pressed by governments. The important thing is to maintain the principle of public announcement of vacancies and open competition.

The difficulty of recruiting staff for the United Nations has steadily increased. All too often nowadays, as the Administrative Committee on Co-ordination has commented, 'the choice is between accepting unsatisfactory standards or leaving posts unfilled'.[145] The general atmosphere of dislocation during the immediate post-war period made it relatively easy at that time to attract competent people into international service. A certain glamour attached to the international organizations. Idealism has not disappeared, but some of the glamour has worn off. Career prospects at the United Nations are not as good as they were. Nationality has been a factor in personnel policy. Salaries are significantly lower than in a number of national services, and it is possible to attract specialists in some fields only by exceeding the normal salary scales. Sudden changes of policy, leading to redundancies, have caused some insecurity and a sagging of staff morale. Every appointment of an insufficiently qualified person depresses the general standard and discourages the more able people from accepting posts in the future.

It is no secret that some governments have been reluctant to release nationals asked for by name by the Secretaries-General. The United Nations cannot afford to manage with less than the best. It is in the interests of all Member States that the Secretariat should reach the highest standards. Although countries can ill afford to spare their most gifted citizens, they are needed in the international secretariats. If all the first-rate people are employed at home, the United Nations will have to get along with second-rate people. Most posts in the Secretariat are highly specialized, and there is only limited demand for the adaptable man or woman of general competence who can usually make a satisfactory career in a national civil service.

It is possible to predict future staff needs in some technical fields. There is a small but continuing demand for statisticians, demographers, agronomists, cartographers, and economists with various kinds of specialization. A limited number of young specialists can be recruited without reference to particular vacancies. Perhaps more could be done on a regional basis, through the various assistance programs, to train persons with a view to future service with international agencies. There should be a progressive expansion of the internship and trainee programs for people from the less-developed areas, in the regions as well as at Headquarters, and every effort should be made to persuade competent interns and trainees to enter into long-term contracts. This may require some system of financial incentives.

An important step forward was taken in 1963 when the Economic and Social Council and the General Assembly, in the context of the United Nations Development Decade, approved the establishment of a United Nations training and research institute, to be financed by voluntary contributions. One of the purposes of the institute is to assist with 'the provision and training of personnel of the highest calibre . . . for national service and service with the United Nations and the specialized agencies . . .'[146]

Recruiting policy must be dynamic. A post can sometimes be filled as a result of public advertisement, inter-agency transfer, or through contacts with professional bodies and governments. But for most professional posts, it is unlikely that candidates offering themselves or suggested by governments will meet all the needs, especially in the higher echelons. Continuous contacts are necessary between the Office of Personnel and appropriate professional associations, academic institutions, and official and semi-official agencies.

In some areas, different international organizations are said to compete for personnel and examine the same applications. Agencies normally inform the others of vacancies, but there is no central registry of openings and applications. The sharing of information and experience between the United Nations and other international agencies, and a positive policy

98

of inter-agency transfers, should be systematically encouraged.
An effective recruiting policy cannot be managed 'on the
cheap'.

There have been a number of suggestions for setting up
an international civil service commission, comparable to national
commissions, for the selection of officials. Those who favour
such a development claim that it would eliminate overlapping
between agencies and would lead to more uniformity of recruiting
policies. Above all, it would make it easier for the executive
heads of the different agencies to resist improper pressures
in personnel matters. The International Civil Service Advisory
Board concluded in 1950 that such an arrangement 'is not
now feasible', though the reasons for this conclusion were
not given.[147] In 1963, however, the Assembly endorsed changes
in the functions and membership of the International Civil
Service Advisory Board itself. Its membership was increased
from nine to eleven, and future appointments will be the subject of consultation between the executive heads of the agencies
and their governing bodies. The Board is to have the services
of a full-time, independent secretary. It has been given authority to foster the development of co-ordination in conditions
of service in the organizations following the United Nations
common system, and its reports will be transmitted by the
Administrative Committee on Co-ordination to the appropriate authorities in each organization. Matters may be referred
to the Board not only by the Administrative Committee on
Co-ordination, but also by the governing or legislative body
of any of the participating organizations.[148]

The International Civil Service Advisory Board, when
reviewing recruitment methods and standards more than a
decade ago, suggested that a pamphlet on employment in the
international secretariats should be prepared.

In order to provide interested persons with general information regarding employment in the international

secretariat (United Nations and the specialized agencies) the Board recommends the early publication of a pamphlet on this subject and its distribution to governments and other institutions where interested persons would normally expect to find such information.[149]

While continued efforts are needed to constitute the Secretariat on a wide geographical basis, these efforts must be subordinate to the absolute necessity of having a Secretariat composed of international officials, responsible only to the Organization, and adhering to the highest standards of performance and integrity. The Secretariat does not become international simply because it is composed of a wide range of nationalities. There should be no place in the Secretariat for officials who cannot give whole-hearted loyalty to the United Nations or whose discretion cannot be relied upon. Hammarskjold rightly insisted:

The Secretariat is international in the way in which it fulfils its functions, not because of its geographic composition but because of the attitudes of the members of the Secretariat and the truly international spirit in which they fulfil their tasks. . . .[150]

APPENDICES

A. Articles of the League of Nations Covenant relating to the Secretariat

Article 2

The action of the League under this Covenant shall be effected through the instrumentality of an Assembly and of a Council, with a permanent Secretariat.

Article 6

1. The permanent Secretariat shall be established at the Seat of the League. The Secretariat shall comprise a Secretary-General and such secretaries and staff as may be required.

2. The first Secretary-General shall be the person named in the Annex; thereafter the Secretary-General shall be appointed by the Council with the approval of the majority of the Assembly.

3. The secretaries and staff of the Secretariat shall be appointed by the Secretary-General with the approval of the Council.

4. The Secretary-General shall act in that capacity at all meetings of the Assembly and of the Council. . . .

Article 7

3. All positions under or in connexion with the League, including the Secretariat, shall be open equally to men and women.

B. Articles of the United Nations Charter relating to the Secretariat

Article 7

    1. There are established as the principal organs of the United Nations: a General Assembly, a Security Council, an Economic and Social Council, a Trusteeship Council, an International Court of Justice, and a Secretariat.

Article 97

    The Secretariat shall comprise a Secretary-General and such staff as the Organization may require. The Secretary-General shall be appointed by the General Assembly upon the recommendation of the Security Council. He shall be the chief administrative officer of the Organization.

Article 98

    The Secretary-General shall act in that capacity in all meetings of the General Assembly, of the Security Council, of the Economic and Social Council, and of the Trusteeship Council, and shall perform such other functions as are entrusted to him by these organs. The Secretary-General shall make an annual report to the General Assembly on the work of the Organization.

Article 99

    The Secretary-General may bring to the attention of the Security Council any matter which in his opinion may threaten the maintenance of international peace and security.

Article 100

    1. In the performance of their duties the Secretary-General and the staff shall not seek or receive instructions from any government or from any other authority external to the Organization. They shall refrain from any action which might reflect on their position as international officials responsible only to the Organization.

    2. Each Member of the United Nations undertakes to respect the exclusively international character of the responsi-

bilities of the Secretary-General and the staff and not to seek to influence them in the discharge of their responsibilities.

Article 101

 1. The staff shall be appointed by the Secretary-General under regulations established by the General Assembly.

 2. Appropriate staffs shall be permanently assigned to the Economic and Social Council, the Trusteeship Council, and, as required, to other organs of the United Nations. These staffs shall form a part of the Secretariat.

 3. The paramount consideration in the employment of the staff and in the determination of the conditions of service shall be the necessity of securing the highest standards of efficiency, competence, and integrity. Due regard shall be paid to the importance of recruiting the staff on as wide a geographical basis as possible.

Article 105

 1. The Organization shall enjoy in the territory of each of its Members such privileges and immunities as are necessary for the fulfilment of its purposes.

 2. Representatives of the Members of the United Nations and officials of the Organization shall similarly enjoy such privileges and immunities as are necessary for the independent exercise of their functions in connection with the Organization.

 3. The General Assembly may make recommendations with a view to determining the details of the application of paragraphs 1 and 2 of this Article or may propose conventions to the Members of the United Nations for this purpose.

C. *Administrative Committee on Co-ordination*[151]

The Administrative Committee on Co-ordination (A.C.C.) which was originally called the Co-ordination Committee, was established under Economic and Social Council Resolution 13 (III) of 21 September 1946. It is entrusted, at the inter-organizational level, with all aspects of co-ordination, including those relating to the common salary system and to personnel policies.

The Council's Resolution noted that the Council, 'being desirous of discharging its responsibility under the Charter of the United Nations to co-ordinate the activities of the United Nations', requested the Secretary-General to establish a standing committee consisting of the executive heads of the United Nations and specialized agencies, 'under the leadership of the Secretary-General to ensure the fullest and most effective implementation of the agreements entered into between the United Nations and the specialized agencies'.

The members of the ACC are the United Nations; International Labour Organization; Food and Agriculture Organization; United Nations Educational, Scientific and Cultural Organization; World Health Organization; International Bank for Reconstruction and Development and its affiliates the International Finance Corporation and the International Development Association; International Monetary Fund; International Civil Aviation Organization; Universal Postal Union; International Telecommunication Union; World Meteorological Organization; Inter-governmental Maritime Consultative Organization; International Atomic Energy Agency; and Interim Commission for the International Trade Organization/General Agreement on Tariffs and Trade.

Ordinarily ACC meets twice a year to consider matters of mutual concern to its members and reports to the Council periodically. It is assisted in its work by a Preparatory Committee of deputies, which reports to it. Among the standing bodies established by ACC to deal with particular fields is its Consultative Committee on Administrative Questions, which consists of the senior officers responsible for administrative and personnel matters in the United Nations and the related agencies. The Consultative Committee on Administrative Questions ordinarily meets once a year to study questions referred to it by ACC or undertaken at its own initiative, and reports to ACC periodically.

D. *International Civil Service Advisory Board*[152]

The origin of the International Civil Service Advisory Board lies in General Assembly resolution 13 (I) of 13 February 1946 under which the Secretary-General was instructed to establish, in consultation with the executive heads of the specialized agencies, an International Civil Service Commission to advise with regard to methods of recruitment and related matters. This question was discussed by a working party of experts of the United Nations and the specialized agencies in April 1947. The title of the body was later changed to 'International Civil Service Advisory Board' to indicate its advisory, as distinguished from an operational or regulatory, character.

The following revised terms of reference were approved in 1963.

a. *Composition*

1. The International Civil Service Advisory Board shall be composed of a Chairman and ten other members appointed by the Secretary-General of the United Nations, with the advice and consent of the Administrative Committee on Coordination.

2. The Board shall be a continuing body. Its members shall normally be appointed for a period of three years. Their terms of office shall expire in rotation, the terms of three, four and four members expiring at the end of each successive year. They shall be eligible for reappointment.

3. Where on a particular matter, the Chairman of the Board is satisfied that action is necessary before the next regular session, the Board shall have authority to act through a panel of three or more of its members, at the discretion of the Chairman.

4. The members of the Board shall be appointed in their personal capacity as individuals who have earned wide public trust for judgment, and whose high qualifications will ensure respect for the Board's advice. They shall be representative of different regions and cultures and bring to the Board diverse experience appropriate to its work. They shall not be chosen or regarded as representatives of organizations.

No Board member shall serve concurrently as a member of the Secretariat of the United Nations or any related agency.

5. Members shall be given allowances adequate to meet their expenses in connexion with Board sessions, including compensation for loss of salary if incurred.

6. The Board shall have a Secretary, appointed by the Secretary-General, with the advice and consent of the Administrative Committee on Co-ordination, after consultation with the Board. The Secretary shall be removable only with the agreement of the Board. In carrying out his duties, he shall be subject only to the instructions of the Board.

b. Functions

7. The functions of the Board shall be:

(1) To advise ACC on

(a) methods of recruitment and the means by which appropriate standards of recruitment may be ensured in the United Nations and the specialized agencies;

(b) aspects of personnel administration related to the recruitment, training and conduct of staff;

(c) such other matters of personnel policy as ACC may refer to it.

(2) To foster the development of co-ordination in conditions of service in the organizations following the United Nations common system, and in particular to review, and make recommendations through ACC on:

(a) the system of classification of posts and its application;

(b) salaries and allowances of staff in the Professional and higher categories;

(c) the methods of and the criteria for establishing the conditions of service of staff in the General Service category and the manner in which the criteria are applied in the Headquarters areas;

(d) divergencies in the application of the common system, the extent to which they should be eliminated, and the manner in which such elimination might be accomplished;

(*e*) any other matter which may be referred to it by ACC (acting either at the request of an executive head or of a legislative or executive authority of an organization in the common system) including:

    (i) the determination of the specific conditions of service of the General Service category in a particular Headquarters area;

    (ii) questions of application and administration of conditions of service in the common system and proposals for changes in the conditions on which the separate organizations concerned have been unable to agree;

    (iii) matters of particular importance to an individual organization, within the general field of personnel administration.

c. Working Arrangements

8. The Board may determine its own procedures. It may request, and to the extent possible shall be given, such information as it requires for the consideration of any matter under examination by it. It shall decide from whom it will receive evidence.

9. The Secretary-General, or other executive head as may be appropriate, shall make available for such periods as may be necessary, such experts, auxiliary staff and facilities as the Board requires for the discharge of its responsibilities.

10. The Board shall normally have one regular session each year. The Chairman may convene supplementary sessions of the full Board, or of a panel of the Board, if he deems that a matter submitted to the Board must be dealt with before the next regular session.

11. The reports of the Board shall be transmitted to the appropriate authorities of each organization through ACC.

d. Budgetary and Financial Arrangements

12. Provisions for the expenses of the Board and its

secretariat shall be included in the budget estimates of the United Nations. In the event that it becomes necessary to hold sessions of the Board, or of a panel of the Board, for which no budgetary provision has been made, the provision of the necessary funds shall be a matter for arrangement between the Chairman and the executive head or heads concerned.

13. The costs of the Board shall be borne by the organizations in a manner to be agreed among them.

E. United Nations Staff Regulations regarding Duties, Obligations, and Privileges[153]

Regulation 1.1 : Members of the Secretariat are international civil servants. Their responsibilities are not national but exclusively international. By accepting appointment, they pledge themselves to discharge their functions and to regulate their conduct with the interests of the United Nations only in view.

Regulation 1.2 : Staff members are subject to the authority of the Secretary-General and to assignment by him to any of the activities or offices of the United Nations. They are responsible to him in the exercise of their functions. The whole time of staff members shall be at the disposal of the Secretary-General. The Secretary-General shall establish a normal working week.

Regulation 1.3 : In the performance of their duties members of the Secretariat shall neither seek nor accept instructions from any government or from any other authority external to the Organization.

Regulation 1.4 : Members of the Secretariat shall conduct themselves at all times in a manner befitting their status as international civil servants. They shall not engage in any activity that is incompatible with the proper discharge of their duties with the United Nations. They shall avoid any action and in particular any kind of public pronouncement which may adversely reflect on their status, or on the integrity, independence and impartiality which are required by that status. While they are not expected to give up their national sentiments or their political and religious convictions, they shall at all times bear in mind the reserve and tact incumbent upon them by reason of their international status.

Regulation 1.5 : Staff members shall exercise the utmost discretion in regard to all matters of official business. They shall not communicate to any person any information known to them by reason of their official position which has not been made public, except in the course of their duties or by authorization of the Secretary-General. Nor shall they at any time use such information to private advantage. These obligations do not cease upon separation from the Secretariat.

Regulation 1.6: No staff member shall accept any honour, decoration, favour, gift or remuneration from any Government excepting for war service; nor shall a staff member accept any honour, decoration, favour, gift or remuneration from any source external to the Organization, without first obtaining the approval of the Secretary-General. Approval shall be granted only in exceptional cases and where such acceptance is not incompatible with the terms of regulation 1.2 of the Staff Regulations and with the individual's status as an international civil servant.

Regulation 1.7: Staff members may exercise the right to vote but shall not engage in any political activity which is inconsistent with or might reflect upon the independence and impartiality required by their status as international civil servants.

Regulation 1.8: The immunities and privileges attached to the United Nations by virtue of Article 105 of the Charter are conferred in the interests of the Organization. These privileges and immunities furnish no excuse to the staff members who enjoy them for non-performance of their private obligations or failure to observe laws and police regulations. In any case where these privileges and immunities arise, the staff member shall immediately report to the Secretary-General, with whom alone it rests to decide whether they shall be waived.

Regulation 1.9: Members of the Secretariat shall subscribe to the following oath or declaration:

'I solemnly swear (undertake, affirm, promise) to exercise in all loyalty, discretion and conscience the functions entrusted to me as an international civil servant of the United Nations, to discharge these functions and regulate my conduct with the interests of the United Nations only in view, and not to seek or accept instructions in regard to the performance of my duties from any government or other authority external to the Organization.'

F. Terms of Reference of the Committee of Experts on the Activities of the Secretariat

General Assembly Resolution 1446 (XIV), 5 December 1959

*   *   *

1. *Requests* the Secretary-General to appoint a committee of experts, composed of six persons with broad and practical experience in the various aspects of administration and chosen with due regard to geographical distribution in consultation with the respective Governments, to work together with the Secretary-General in reviewing the activities and organization of the Secretariat of the United Nations with a view to effecting or proposing further measures designed to ensure maximum economy and efficiency in the Secretariat;

2. *Requests* the Secretary-General to consult with the Advisory Committee on Administrative and Budgetary Questions on the arrangements to be made under paragraph 1 above;

3. *Requests* the Secretary-General, having considered a report of the committee of experts, to present to the General Assembly at its fifteenth session provisional recommendations thereon together with the committee's report, bearing in mind that the Secretary-General's final recommendations together with further reports of the committee shall be presented to the General Assembly at its sixteenth session;

4. *Requests* the Advisory Committee on Administrative and Budgetary Questions to submit its observations on the review and on the reports of the Secretary-General.

General Assembly Resolution 1557 (XV), 18 December 1960

*   *   *

2. *Confirms* the provisional decision of the Secretary-General that, notwithstanding the provisions of paragraph 1 of the General Assembly resolution 1446 (XIV) of 5 December 1959, the composition of the Committee of Experts should be increased from six to eight members. . . .

General Assembly Resolution 1559 (XV), 18 December 1960

*　　　*　　　*

1. *Requests* the Committee of Experts appointed by General Assembly resolution 1446 (XIV) of 5 December 1959 to study the categories of posts subject to geographical distribution and the criteria for determining the range of posts for each Member State with a view to securing a wide geographical distribution of the staff of the Secretariat, taking into account *inter alia*, the relative importance of various posts, and to report to the Assembly at its sixteenth session. . . .

A NOTE ON FURTHER READING

The main sources on the U.N. Secretariat are the reports of the Secretary-General, the Advisory Committee on Administrative and Budgetary Questions, the International Civil Service Advisory Board, and the Committee of Experts on the Activities and Organization of the Secretariat (1960/1), and the debates in the General Assembly (Fifth Committee and plenary). In addition the following works in English may be consulted:

Hammarskjold, Dag. *The International Civil Servant in Law and in Fact*. Oxford, Clarendon Press, 1961.

Langrod, Georges. *The International Civil Service*. Leyden, Sythoff, 1963.

Lie, Trygve. *In the Cause of Peace*. New York, Macmillan, 1954.

Loveday, Alexander. *Reflections on International Administration*. Oxford, Clarendon Press, 1956.

Ranshofen-Wertheimer, Egon F. *The International Secretariat: a great experiment in international administration*. Washington, Carnegie Endowment for International Peace, 1945.

Schwebel, Stephen M. *The Secretary-General of the United Nations*. Cambridge (Mass.), Harvard University Press, 1952.

Scott, F. R. 'The World's Civil Service', *International Conciliation* No. 496, Carnegie Endowment for International Peace, 1954.

The Internal Administration of an International Secretariat. London, Royal Institute of International Affairs, 1945.

The International Secretariat of the Future. London, Royal Institute of International Affairs, 1944.

The United Nations Secretariat. New York, Carnegie Endowment for International Peace, 1950.

REFERENCES

1. G.A.O.R., 17th Session, Supplement No. 1A (August 1962, p. 5); 18th Session, Supplement No. 1A (20 August 1963), p. 6.
2. Articles 12 and 11 (2) of the Charter.
3. I.C.J. Reports 1962, p. 163.
4. G.A.O.R., 16th Session, Supplement No. 1A (17 August 1961), pp. 3–4.
5. Articles 2, 6 (1–4), and 7(3) of the League of Nations Covenant.
6. *Proceedings of the Exploratory Conference on the Experience of the League of Nations Secretariat*, Washington, Carnegie Endowment for International Peace, 1942 (mimeographed), p. 41.
7. Report of the Committee of Enquiry on the Organization of the Secretariat, the International Labour Office and the Registry of the Permanent Court of International Justice. Geneva, League of Nations, 28 June 1930, A.16.1930.
8. Ibid, Appendix II, pp. 29–31.
9. Article 11 (1) of the League of Nations Covenant.
10. Documents of the United Nations Conference on International Organization. New York and London, U.N. Information Org., 1945, Vol. III, pp. 491, 595; Vol. VII, pp. 175–7, 510, 511.
11. Staff Regulation 1.9.
12. G.A.O.R., 7th Session, Annexes, Agenda item 75, A/2364 (30 January 1953), para. 8; see also Dag Hammarskjold, *The International Civil Servant in Law and in Fact*, Oxford, Clarendon Press, 1961, p. 16.
13. United Nations Preparatory Commission, Committee 6, 22nd and 23rd meetings, PC/AB/66 (19 and 20 December 1945).

14. See, for example, G.A.O.R., 16th Session, 5th Committee, 873rd meeting (7 November 1961), para 44; 875th meeting (8 November 1961), para. 5; 17th Session, 5th Committee, 928th meeting (23 October 1962), para 47; 18th Session, 5th Committee, 1034th meeting (6 November 1963).
15. G.A.O.R., 16th Session, 5th Committee, 872nd meeting (6 November 1961), para. 4; 874th meeting (8 November 1961), para. 31.
16. G.A.O.R., 7th Session, 413th plenary meeting (10 March 1953), para. 19.
17. Hammarskjold, *The International Civil Servant in Law and in Fact*, pp. 16–17; see also Trygve Lie, *In the Cause of Peace*, New York, Macmillan, 1954, pp. 386–405.
18. G.A.O.R., 7th Session, Annexes, Agenda item 75, A/2364 (30 January 1953); G.A. res. 708 (VII), 1 April 1953.
19. G.A.O.R., 12th Session, 5th Committee, 629th meeting (27 November 1957), para. 3; 18th Session, 5th Committee, 1041st meeting (14 November 1963).
20. Staff Regulation 1.4.
21. Report on Standards of Conduct in the International Civil Service, International Civil Service Advisory Board, COORD/CIVIL SERVICE/5 (1954), para 4; see also G.A.O.R., 8th Session, Annexes, Agenda item 51, A/2533 (21 November 1953), para. 59.
22. See Staff Regulation 1.5.
23. G.A.O.R., 7th Session, Annexes, Agenda item 75, A/2364 (30 January 1953), para. 24; see also Report on Standards of Conduct in the International Civil Service, para 8, and Report on In-Service Training in the United Nations and the Specialized Agencies, International Civil Service Advisory Board, COORD/CIVIL SERVICE/4 (1952), para. 7.
24. Staff Regulation 1.4.
25. Press conference at U.N. Headquarters, 12 June 1961, Note to Correspondents No. 2347, p. 11.
26. *The International Secretariat of the Future*, London, Royal Institute of International Affairs, 1944, p. 18.
27. Staff Regulation 1.2.
28. G.A.O.R., 16th Session, 5th Committee, 869th meeting (1 November 1961), para. 51.

29. G.A.O.R., 18th Session, 5th Committee, 1038th meeting (12 November 1963).
30. Source: G.A.O.R., 18th Session, Annexes, Agenda item 66, A/C.5/987 (11 October 1963).
31. U.N. doc. A/3209 (18 October 1956), para. 54.
32. G.A.O.R., 11th Session, Annexes, Agenda item 51, A/3558 (25 February 1957), para. 128; G.A. res. 1095 (XI), 27 February 1957.
33. G.A.O.R., 16th Session, Annexes, Agenda item 61, A/4776 (14 June 1961), para. 92.
34. G.A.O.R., 16th Session, Annexes, Agenda item 64, A/5063 (18 December 1961), para. 37.
35. G.A.O.R., 18th Session, Annexes, Agenda item 66, A/C. 5/987 (11 October 1963), para. 18.
36. Report of the Preparatory Commission of the United Nations, PC/20 (23 December 1945), Chap. VIII, Sec. 2, para. 16, pp. 86–87.
37. Lie, *In the Cause of Peace*, p. 39.
38. *The International Secretariat of the Future*, p. 8.
39. Report of the Preparatory Commission of the United Nations, PC/20 (23 December 1945), Chap. VIII, Sec. 2, para. 16, pp. 86–87.
40. G.A.O.R., 5th Session, 289th plenary meeting (28 September 1950), para. 40.
41. S.C.O.R., 11th year, 751st meeting (31 October 1956), para. 1.
42. S.C.O.R., 14th year, 847th meeting (7 September 1959), para. 12.
43. S.C.O.R., 15th year, 873rd meeting (13/14 July 1960), para. 26.
44. Michel Virally, 'Le rôle politique du Secrétaire-Général des Nations Unies', Annuaire Français de Droit International, Paris, Centre National de la Recherche Scientifique, 1958, pp. 369–70.
45. S.C.O.R., 16th year, 964th meeting (28 July 1961), para. 86.
46. In 1958, for example, when the General Assembly was considering the future of United Nations assistance to Palestine refugees, a specific request that the Secretary-General should submit proposals on the matter was withdrawn on the understanding that the Secretary-General would, 'as part of his regular duties, look into the technical

operation of UNRWA in preparation of such proposals as he might consider helpful or necessary to bring forward to the General Assembly. . . .' G.A.O.R., 13th Session, Special Political Committee, 125th meeting (10 December 1958), para. 5.

47. G.A.O.R., 12th Session, 690th plenary meeting (26 September 1957), paras. 72–73.

48. S.C.O.R., 13th year, 837th meeting (22 July 1958), paras. 10–16.

49. G.A.O.R., 14th Session, Supplement No. 1A, p. 3.

50. U.N. doc. SG/868, 8 November 1959.

51. Soviet Mission to the U.N., Press Release, 16 November 1959.

52. G.A.O.R., 17th Session, Annexes, Agenda item 89, A/5170 (20 August 1962).

53. U.N. docs. S/5298 (29 April 1963), S/5321 (27 May 1963), S/5326 (8 June 1963).

54. U.N. doc. SG/1583, 13 September 1963.

55. Speech in Chicago, U.N. doc. SG/910, 1 May 1960, p. 6.

56. Hammarskjold, *The International Civil Service in Law and in Fact*, p. 11.

57. The main statements of the Soviet position are to be found in Khrushchev's speeches in plenary meetings of the General Assembly, G.A.O.R., 15th Session, 869th, 882nd, and 904th plenary meetings (23 September, 3 October, and 13 October 1960); in part of a draft resolution on disarmament submitted to the First Committee, G.A.O.R., 15th Session, Annexes, Agenda items 67, 86, 69 and 73, A/C.1/L.249 (13 October 1960); in the statement of the Soviet Government that it would 'not maintain any relations with Hammarskjold and . . . not recognize him as an official of the United Nations . . .', S.C.O.R., 16th year, Supplement for January, February and March, S/4704 (14 February 1961); and in the views expressed by the Soviet member of the Committee of Experts on the Activities and Organization of the Secretariat, G.A.O.R., 16th Session, Annexes, Agenda item 61, A/4776 (14 June 1961), pp. 41–42.

58. G.A.O.R., 15th Session, 869th plenary meeting (23 September 1960), paras. 283–5.

59. See, for example, G.A.O.R., 16th Session, 5th Committee, 874th meeting (8 November 1961), paras. 27, 29, 32.
60. See King Gordon, *The United Nations in the Congo*, New York, Carnegie Endowment for International Peace, 1962.
61. G.A.O.R., 1st Emergency Special Session, Agenda item 5, A/3302 (6 November 1956), para. 8; 13th Session, Annexes, Agenda item 65, A/3943 (9 October 1958), paras. 166–7.
62. S.C.O.R., 15th year, Supplement for July, August and September, S/4426 (9 August 1960), para. 4.
63. S.C.O.R., 15th year, Supplement for July, August and September, S/4503 and S/4475/Add. 2.
64. G.A.O.R., 15th Session, 869th plenary meeting (23 September 1960), paras. 278–9.
65. G.A.O.R., 15th Session, 882nd plenary meeting (3 October 1960), paras. 48–49. Khrushchev told C. L. Sulzberger that 'The "troika" principle will be necessary only in the event that international forces are set up. The command of these forces should be based on that principle. This would be necessary to guarantee that no state or group of states could use international United Nations forces to the detriment of any other state of group of states.' *The New York Times*, 8 September 1961.
66. G.A.O.R., 15th Session, 869th plenary meeting (23 September 1960), para. 285.
67. U.N. doc. A/4797 (7 July 1961), p. 8.
68. See the statement by the Rapporteur in Report of the Committee of Experts . . ., Appendix 2.
69. S.C.O.R., 15th year, 887th meeting (21 August 1960).
70. S.C.O.R., 16th year, 935th meeting (15 February 1961), para. 35.
71. Hammarskjold, *The International Civil Servant in Law and in Fact*, p. 23; see also G.A.O.R., 16th Session, Supplement No. 1A, p. 5.
72. See, for example, S.C.O.R., 16th year, Supplement for October, November and December, S/5003 (27 November, 1961).
73. Egon F. Ranshofen-Wertheimer, *The International Secretariat: a Great Experiment in International Administration*, Washington, Carnegie Endowment for International Peace, 1945, pp. 73–74.

74. *Proceedings of the Exploratory Conference on the Experience of the League of Nations*, pp. 40, 41, 45.

75. See Sydney D. Bailey, *British Parliamentary Democracy*, Boston, Houghton Mifflin (London, Harrap), second edition, 1962, pp. 210–11.

76. Source: G.A.O.R., 18th Session, Supplement No. 5 (1963), pp. 19, 37–48, 116, 120, 125–7.

77. G.A.O.R., 16th Session, Annexes, Agenda item 61, A/4776 (14 June 1961). This document is hereafter cited as 'Report of the Committee of Experts . . .'

78. G.A.O.R., 14th Session, Supplement No. 7 (1959), para 41.

79. G.A. res. 1446 (XIV) 5 December 1959. For the terms of reference of the Committee, see Appendix F pp. 112–13.

80. Report of the Committee of Experts . . ., Appendix 2.

81. G.A. res. 1446 (XIV), 5 December 1959.

82. G.A.O.R., 16th Session, Annexes, Agenda item 61, A/4794 (30 June 1961), para. 2. This document is hereafter cited as 'Comments of the Secretary-General . . .'

83. Report of the Committee of Experts . . ., Annex 1.

84. Documents of the United Nations Conference on International Organization. New York and London, U.N. Information Org., 1945, Vol. III, p. 627, and Vol. VII, pp. 203–5, 280–1.

85. G.A. res. 13 (1), 13 February 1946.

86. Lie, *In the Cause of Peace*, pp. 45–50.

87. Ibid., p. 47.

88. G.A.O.R., 7th Session, Annexes, Agenda item 69, A/2214 (7 October 1952).

89. Lie, *In the Cause of Peace*, p. 43.

90. G.A. res. 13 (1), 13 February 1946.

91. G.A.O.R., 12th Session, Annexes, Agenda item 41, A/C.5/728 (7 November 1957), para. 18.

92. G.A.O.R., 12th Session, Annexes, Agenda item 41, A/3762 (3 December 1957), para. 20; 5th Committee, 641st meeting (10 December 1957), para. 4.

93. G.A.O.R., 15th Session, 896th plenary meeting (10 October 1960), para. 80.

94. Report of the Committee of Experts . . ., para. 37.

95. Ibid., para. 35 and Appendix I (italics added). See also G.A.O.R., 17th Session, 5th Committee, 951st meeting

(19 November 1962), para. 1; 18th Session, 5th Committee, 1037th meeting (11 November 1962).

96. Report of the Committee of Experts . . ., paras. 38–41.
97. Comments of the Secretary-General . . ., paras. 6–30.
98. U.N. doc. SG/1040, 26 June 1961.
99. Comments of the Secretary-General . . ., para. 20; Report of the Committee of Experts . . ., Annex 1, para. 36.
100. G.A.O.R., 16th Session, 1046th plenary meeting (3 November 1961), para. 30; 5th Committee, 894th meeting (4 December 1961), para. 42; U.N. doc. SG/1102, 29 December 1961.
101. G.A.O.R., 3rd Session, Annexes, Agenda item 40, A/652 (2 September 1948), para. 7.
102. Sources: G.A.O.R., 3rd Session, Annexes, Agenda item 40, A/652 (2 September 1948), Annex 2; 18th Session, Annexes, Agenda item 66, A/C.5/987 (11 October 1963).
103. G.A.O.R., 12th Session, 5th Committee, 630th meeting (28 November 1957), para. 62.
104. Report on Recruitment Methods and Standards for the United Nations and the Specialized Agencies, International Civil Service Advisory Board, COORD/CIVIL SERVICE/2/Rev. 1 (1950), para. 10 (i).
105. G.A.O.R., 16th Session, 5th Committee, 872nd meeting (6 November 1961), para. 31.
106. Polish Mission to the U.N., Press Release. The provisional summary record of the meeting gives the same sense, but the meaning is slightly amended in G.A.O.R., 16th Session, 5th Committee, 860th meeting (30 October 1961), para. 29.
107. G.A.O.R., 2nd Session, 5th Committee, 82nd meeting (30 October 1947), pp. 291–2; 91st meeting (7 November 1947), p. 372.
108. G.A.O.R., 3rd Session, Annexes, Agenda item 40, A/652 (2 September 1948), paras. 8–10 and Annex 1.
109. Report of the Committee of Experts . . ., para. 74.
110. 'I do not consider the formula recommended by the majority an ideal formula, but when it was first proposed by the Soviet expert . . .' Separate opinion by Francisco Urrutia, Report of the Committee of Experts . . ., Appendix 2.
111. G.A.O.R., 16th Session, 5th Committee, 864th meeting

(25 October 1961), para. 20; 869th meeting (1 November 1961), para. 52; 871st meeting (3 November 1961), paras. 13 and 31; 872nd meeting (6 November 1961), para. 29; 873rd meeting (7 November 1961), para. 43.

112. G.A.O.R., 16th Session, Annexes, Agenda item 64, A/5063 (18 December 1961), Annexes 1 and 11.

113. G.A.O.R., 16th Session, 5th Committee, 863rd meeting (24 October 1961), para. 36; 890th meeting (27 November 1961), para. 23; 908th meeting (18 December 1961), paras. 68–71.

114. G.A.O.R., 17th Session, Annexes, Agenda item 70, A/5270 (24 October 1962), para. 69b.

115. G.A. res. 1852 (XVII), 19 December 1962.

116. G.A.O.R., 18th Session, Annexes, Agenda item 66, A/C.5/987 (11 October 1963), para. 6.

117. Source: G.A.O.R., 17th Session, Annexes, Agenda item 70, A/5270 (24 October 1962), para. 8; 18th Session, Annexes, Agenda item 66, A/C.5/987 (11 October 1963), para. 9.

118. Source: G.A.O.R., 18th Session, Annexes, Agenda item 66, A/C.5/987 (11 October 1963), Tables B and F.

119. Source: G.A.O.R., 18th Session, Annexes, Agenda item 66, A/C.5/987 (11 October 1963), Tables II, V, VI, and VII.

120. Report of the Committee of Experts . . ., para. 70.

121. Report on Recruitment Methods and Standards for the United Nations and the Specialized Agencies, para. 18.

122. G.A.O.R., 17th Session, Annexes, Agenda item 70, A/5270 (24 October 1962), paras. 55–64.

123. G.A. res. 1852 (XVII), 19 December 1962.

124. G.A.O.R., 18th Session, Annexes, Agenda item 66, A/C.5/987 (11 October 1963), para. 15.

125. G.A.O.R., 15th Session, Annexes, Agenda item 60, A/C.5/833 (17 October 1960), para. 2.

126. G.A. res. 1559 (XV), 18 December 1960.

127. Report of the Committee of Experts . . ., para. 53; Comments of the Secretary-General . . ., para. 40.

128. G.A.O.R., 17th Session, Annexes, Agenda item 70, A/C.5/933 (24th October 1962), paras. 40–54.

129. G.A.O.R., 17th Session, Annexes, Agenda item 70, A/5377 (18 December 1962), para. 36.

130. G.A.O.R., 18th Session, 5th Committee, 1038th meeting

(12 November 1963); 1040th meeting (14 November 1963); 1041st meeting (14 November 1963).

131. Report of the Committee of Experts . . ., para. 57.
132. Report of the Committee of Experts . . ., para. 56; see also G.A.O.R., 18th Session, 5th Committee, 1038th meeting (12 November 1963); 1040th meeting (14 November 1963).
133. G.A.O.R., 17th Session, Annexes, Agenda item 70, A/5270 (24 October 1962), para. 39.
134. G.A. res. 1852 (XVII), 19 December 1962.
135. Source: G.A.O.R., 18th Session, Annexes, Agenda item 66, A/C.5/987 (11 October 1963), para. 22.
136. G.A.O.R., 16th Session, 5th Committee, 851st meeting (9 October 1961), para. 16; 872nd meeting (6 November 1961), para. 14.
137. Source; ECOSOC Official Records, 36th Session, Supplement No. 5 (8 May 1963), Annex VIII.
138. Report of the Committee of Experts . . ., paras. 86 and 89.
139. Report of the Preparatory Commission of the United Nations. PC/20 (23 December 1945), Chap. VIII, Sec. 2, para. 60, p. 92.
140. G.A.O.R., 14th Session, Annexes, Agenda item 54, A/C.5/784 (1 October 1959), para. 12.
141. Article 6 (3) of the League of Nations Covenant.
142. Staff Regulation 4.1.
143. See Appendix D, pp. 106–9.
144. *The Internal Administration of an International Secretariat*, London, Royal Institute of International Affairs, 1945, pp. 25–26; see also *The International Secretariat of the Future*, p. 25.
145. G.A.O.R., 16th Session, Annexes, Agenda item 65, A/C.5/L.685 (8 November 1961), Annex, para. 2.
146. ECOSOC res. 985 (XXXVI), 2 August 1963; G.A. res. 1934 (XVIII), 11 December 1963.
147. Report on Recruitment Methods and Standards for the United Nations and the Specialized Agencies, para. 28.
148. G.A. res. 1981 (XVIII), 17 December 1963. For the revised terms of reference of the Board, see Appendix D, pp. 106–9.
149. Report on Recruitment Methods and Standards for the United Nations and the Specialized Agencies, para. 39.

150. G.A.O.R., 15th Session, Annexes, Agenda item 50, A/C.5/843 (21 November 1960), para. 10.

151. G.A.O.R., 18th Session, Annexes, Agenda item 64, A/C.5/L.804 (11 November 1963).

152. G.A.O.R., 18th Session, Annexes, Agenda item 64, A/C.5/L.804 (11 November 1963) and A/C.5/976 (23 July 1963).

153. U.N. doc. ST/SGB/Staff Rules/1, 16 March 1962.

INDEX